First School Dictionary

Illustrated by
Stephanie Strickland

Collins

Collins First School Dictionary

First published 2000

© HarperCollins*Publishers* Ltd 2000

10 9 8 7 6 5 4 3 2 1

ISBN 0 00 316153 6 hardback
ISBN 0 00 316154 4 paperback

A catalogue record for this book is available from the British Library.

Published by Collins
A division of HarperCollins*Publishers* Ltd
77–85 Fulham Palace Road
Hammersmith
London W6 8JB

www.CollinsEducation.com
On-line Support for Schools and Colleges

www.fireandwater.com
Visit the book lover's website

Compilers   Jock Graham, Marie Lister

Literacy consultants   Kay Hiatt, Ginny Lapage
Numeracy consultant   Jan Henley
Science consultant   Rona Wyn Davies

Cover designer   Susi Martin
Design   Perry Tate Design
Illustrators   Stephanie Strickland,
                           Sebastian Quigley (pp. 172–5)

Photos
All commissioned photos by Steve Lumb.

The publishers wish to thank the following for permission to use photographs:
Art Directors & Trip: p. 7 aeroplane, p. 28 castle, p. 59 flower, p. 61 frog, p. 78 jigsaw, p. 94 moon, p. 155 tongue, p. 171 zip; **Biofotos/Heather Angel**: p. 70 hedgehog; **Holt Studios**: p. 23 bud; **ICCE**: p. 49 Earth; **Oxford Scientific Films**: p. 14 badger, p. 27 carrot, p. 60 fossil, p. 63 gerbil, p. 81 koala, p. 87 lizard, p. 105 panda, p. 107 peacock, p. 108 penguin, p. 111 plum, p. 120 raspberries, p. 168 wolf; **Papilio**: p. 6 acorn, p. 8 alligator, p. 10 antelope, p. 16 basket, p. 18 biscuits, p. 19 blackbird, p. 32 cliff, p. 33 coconut; **Tony Stone Images**: p. 12 astronaut, p. 30 chimpanzee, p. 39 crocodile, p. 111 plaster, p. 159 twins, p. 169 wrinkles; **John Walmsley**: p. 144 statue.

All other photos and illustrations © HarperCollins*Publishers* Ltd 2000.

Acknowledgements
The publishers would also like to thank all the teachers, staff and pupils who contributed to this book:

Models
Kayla Castello
Stacey Cleary
Tom Crane
Katherine Davis
William Davis
Nicki Denaro and Mauri-Joy Smith
Elizabeth Fison
Jesse Johnson

Ismael Khan
Lindsay Linehan
Guy Orridge
Zina Patel
Thomas Permaul-Baker
Tom Symonds
Lara Walters

Schools
Aberhill Primary, Fife; ASDAC, Fife; Canning St Primary, Newcastle upon Tyne; Cowgate Primary, Newcastle upon Tyne; Crombie Primary, Fife; the Literacy Team at Dryden Professional Development Centre, Gateshead; Dunshalt Primary, Fife; Ecton Brook Lower, Northampton; English Martyrs RC Primary, Newcastle upon Tyne; Hotspur Primary, Newcastle upon Tyne; John Betts Primary, London; Lemington First, Newcastle upon Tyne; Literacy Centre, Newcastle upon Tyne; LMTC Education Development Centre, Northumberland; Melcombe Primary, London; Methilhill Primary, Fife; Northampton High, Northampton; Pitcoudie Primary, Fife; Pitreavie Primary, Fife; Ravenswood Primary, Newcastle upon Tyne; St Andrew's CE Primary, London; Simon de Senlis Lower, Northampton; Sinclairtown Primary, Fife; Standens Barn Lower, Northampton; Touch Primary, Fife; Towcester Infants, Northampton; Wooton Primary, Northampton.

Printed in Great Britain by Scotprint Book Printers, Haddington, East Lothian

Contents

Using this dictionary

A **dictionary** tells you what a word means and how to spell it. The words in a dictionary are in alphabetical order.

How to find a word

Look for the word "hamster". What letter does it begin with?

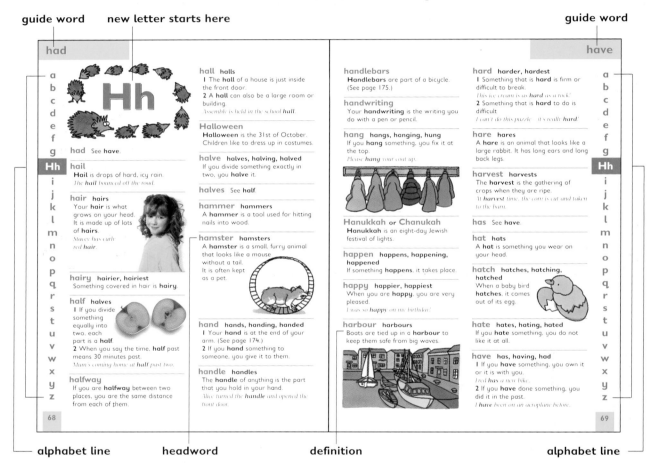

You can find the letter "h" in three places:

1 Each new letter starts with **big letters at the top** of the page.

2 Look at the **alphabet line** on the side of the page. This helps you remember alphabetical order, from **a** to **z**. The pink box shows you that the words on this page start with "h".

3 Look at the **guide word** at the top of each page. These are the first and last words on these pages. Here, the first word is "had" and the last word is "have". Do these words start with the same letter as "hamster"?

When you find the right page, look at the blue words. These are called **headwords**. The headwords are in alphabetical order. Find "hamster".

Look at the **definition** under the headword. The definition tells you what the word means.

The **headword** is the word that you are looking up.

The **definition** tells you what the word means.

This word has **more than one meaning**.

Some definitions have an **example sentence**. This shows you how the word can be used.

Next to the word you will see how to spell the **plural or other forms** of the word.

A photograph or **illustration** tells you more about what the word means.

Some definitions tell you **where to find out more**.

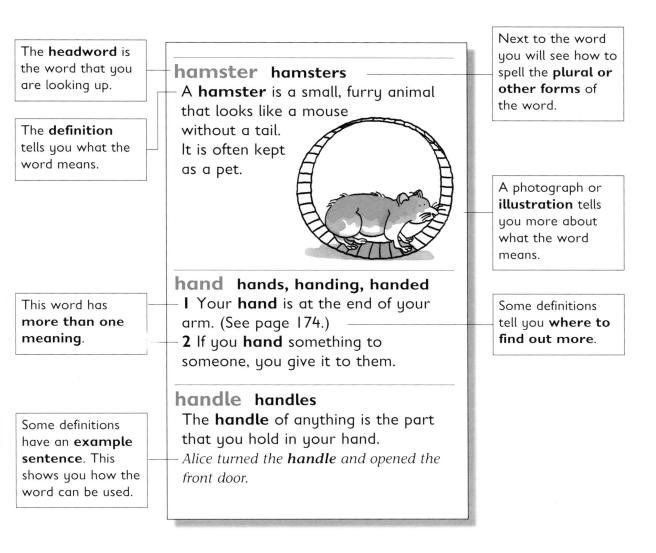

hamster **hamsters**
A **hamster** is a small, furry animal that looks like a mouse without a tail. It is often kept as a pet.

hand **hands, handing, handed**
1 Your **hand** is at the end of your arm. (See page 174.)
2 If you **hand** something to someone, you give it to them.

handle **handles**
The **handle** of anything is the part that you hold in your hand.
Alice turned the handle and opened the front door.

Picture pages, word banks and number banks

This dictionary also has special pages at the back.

Picture pages have **illustrations with labels**. Labels tell you what something is called. The labels at the back of this book tell you the names of dinosaurs, parts of the body, parts of a bicycle, parts of a car and clothes.

Word banks and number banks help you learn and spell time words, question words, synonyms and antonyms, shapes and colours.

Aa

b c d e f g h i j k l m n o p q r s t u v w x y z

abacus abacuses

An **abacus** is a counting frame with beads that move on wires or rods.

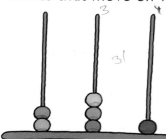

The number of beads for this abacus shows us the size of the number. This number has 2 hundreds, 3 tens and 1 unit. It is 231.

able

When you can do something, you are **able** to do it.

I am able to read this book now.

about

1 About means to do with.
My book is about Africa.
2 About also means not exactly.
I'll be home at about 6 o'clock.

accident accidents

An **accident** is something which happens that was not planned.
The car slid on the ice, causing an accident.
Mum broke the cup by accident.

ache aches

An **ache** is a pain that goes on hurting, like toothache.
I have had an ache in my leg all day.

acorn acorns

An **acorn** is a small nut that grows on an oak tree. Oak trees grow from **acorns**.

act acts, acting, acted

1 You **act** when you do something.
The doctor acted quickly to save his life.
2 When you pretend to be someone in a play or film, you are **acting**.

active

An **active** person is full of life and is doing something.

actor actors

An **actor** is a man or woman who acts in a play or a film.

actress actresses

A female actor is sometimes called an **actress**.

add adds, adding, added

1 If you **add** one thing to another, you put it with something else.
2 If you **add** numbers, you find out how many they make altogether.
The symbol + means **add**.
One add one makes two. 1 + 1 = 2

addition

Addition is what you do when you add numbers or other things together.

address addresses
Your **address** is where you live.
My address is 15 Castle Street, Dover.

adjective adjectives
An **adjective** is a word that describes a person or thing.

The little girl lived in an old house.

adjectives

adult adults
An **adult** is a grown-up person.

adventure adventures
You have an **adventure** when something exciting happens to you.

adverb adverbs
An **adverb** is a word that tells you more about a verb.

The wind blew wildly.

adverb

aeroplane aeroplanes
An **aeroplane** is a flying machine that carries people and things.

afraid
When you are **afraid**, you are scared or frightened.

after
Something that is **after** something else is later than it.
I watch television after school.

afternoon afternoons
The **afternoon** is the part of the day between 12 noon and evening.

again
If you do something **again**, you do it once more.
Sarah rang the bell and then she rang it again.

against
1 If you put a ladder **against** a wall, you put it so close that it touches the wall.
2 If you are playing **against** a team, you are on the other side.

age ages
Your **age** is the number of years you have lived.

ago
Ago means in the past.
Joe started school two years ago.

Aa

b
c
d
e
f
g
h
i
j
k
l
m
n
o
p
q
r
s
t
u
v
w
x
y
z

agree **agrees, agreeing, agreed**
When you **agree** with someone, you think the same as they do.
*The girls **agreed** to go swimming.*

air
Air is made of gases. It is all around but you cannot see it. People must breathe **air** to live.

airport **airports**
Aeroplanes land and take off at an **airport**.

alien **aliens**
An **alien** is a creature from another planet.
*The **aliens** arrived in a spaceship.*

alike
People or things that are nearly the same are **alike**.
*Arun and Ram look **alike** because they are brothers.*

alive
When people, animals and plants are living, they are **alive**.

all
1 All means each member or part.
All my family came to the wedding.
2 All also means the whole of something.
*Liz ate **all** the jelly.*

alligator **alligators**
An **alligator** is a scaly reptile that looks like a crocodile. It lives on land and in water.

alliteration
Using words which begin with the same sound closely together is called **alliteration**.
*"Green grass" is an example of **alliteration**.*

allow **allows, allowing, allowed**
When you **allow** someone to do something, you let them do it.
*Kate **allowed** Peter to use her ruler.*

almost
Almost means nearly but not quite.
*It was **almost** 3 o'clock.*

alone
You are **alone** if there is nobody with you.

aloud
When you read **aloud**, people can hear you.

alphabet **alphabets**
An **alphabet** is all the letters used in writing, set out in a special order.
There is an **alphabet** down the side of this page.

alphabetical
Alphabetical means in the same order as the letters of the alphabet.
*The words in this dictionary are listed in **alphabetical** order.*

already
Already means before now.
*I have **already** had my dinner.*

also
Also means as well.
*I can swim and dive. I can **also** skate.*

altogether
When you add things up, the answer is what you have **altogether**.
*Rasheed has four stickers and Anna has five, so they have nine stickers **altogether**.*

always
If something **always** happens, it happens every time.
*This bus is **always** late.*

amazing
If something is **amazing**, you are filled with a feeling of great surprise.

ambulance ambulances
An **ambulance** is a special van that takes sick people to hospital.

amount amounts
The **amount** of something is how much of it there is.
*There was a huge **amount** of snow on the road.*

amphibian amphibians
An **amphibian** is an animal that lives part of its life in water and part on the land. A frog is an **amphibian**.

analogue
The face of an **analogue** clock or watch has numbers from 1 to 12. Two hands point to the numbers to tell you the time.

ancient
Ancient means very old or long ago.
*The Pyramids were built in **ancient** times.*

angry angrier, angriest
If you are very annoyed and upset, you feel **angry**.

animal animals
An **animal** is a living creature that is not a plant. For example, dogs, birds, fish, insects and people are **animals**.

ankle ankles
Your **ankle** is the part of your leg that joins your foot.
(See page 174.)

Aa
b
c
d
e
f
g
h
i
j
k
l
m
n
o
p
q
r
s
t
u
v
w
x
y
z

b
c
d
e
f
g
h
i
j
k
l
m
n
o
p
q
r
s
t
u
v
w
x
y
z

anniversary anniversaries
An **anniversary** is a date you remember each year because something special happened on it.
*The 25th of May is my grandparents' wedding **anniversary**.*

announce announces, announcing, announced
When you **announce** something, you say it aloud to let everyone know.
*Miss Jones **announced** the winner.*

annoy annoys, annoying, annoyed
If you **annoy** someone, you make them angry.

another
1 Another means one more.
*Can I have **another** cake?*
2 Another can also mean different.
*Try to do the sum **another** way.*

answer answers, answering, answered
1 If you **answer**, you speak to someone who has just spoken to you.
2 You give an **answer** when somebody asks you a question.

ant ants
An **ant** is a tiny insect. **Ants** live in large groups.

antelope antelopes
An **antelope** is a wild animal from Africa that looks like a deer. It can run very fast.

anticlockwise
If you go **anticlockwise**, you move in the opposite direction to the hands of a clock.

antonym antonyms
An **antonym** is a word that means the opposite of another word. Hot is the **antonym** of cold. Fast is an **antonym** of slow. (See page 181.)

anxious
If you are **anxious**, you are worried about something.

any
1 Any means one, some or a few.
*Have you got **any** crisps?*
2 Any also means whichever you want.
*I'm not busy, so you can come **any** day.*

anybody
Anybody means any person.

anyone
Anyone is another word for anybody.

anything
Anything means any thing at all.

anywhere
Anywhere means in any place at all.
*I'll meet you **anywhere** you like.*

apart

If something falls **apart**, it falls to pieces.

ape apes

An **ape** is a monkey without a tail. Gorillas and chimpanzees are **apes**.

apologize or apologise
apologizes, apologizing, apologized

If you **apologize**, you say you are sorry for something you have done.
Sue apologized for being late.

appear appears, appearing, appeared

When something **appears**, you can suddenly see it.

apple apples

An **apple** is a round, juicy fruit that grows on a tree. Its skin can be red, green or yellow.

April

April is the fourth month of the year. It has 30 days.

apron aprons

You wear an **apron** over your clothes to stop them getting dirty when you paint or cook.

arch arches

An **arch** is part of a building or bridge. It has a curved top and straight sides.

area areas

An **area** is a part of a country or place.
*This park has a special **area** for dogs.*

argue argues, arguing, argued

If you **argue** with someone, you quarrel with them.

argument arguments

An **argument** happens when people argue.

arm arms

Your **arm** is a part of your body. It is between your hand and your shoulder. (See page 174.)

armour

Armour is metal clothing or plates worn to protect the body.
*Long ago, soldiers wore suits of **armour**.*

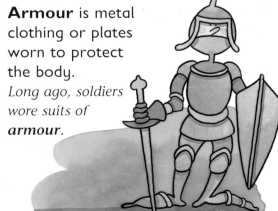

Aa

b
c
d
e
f
g
h
i
j
k
l
m
n
o
p
q
r
s
t
u
v
w
x
y
z

army armies
An **army** is a large group of soldiers trained to fight on land.

arrange arranges, arranging, arranged
1 If you **arrange** to do something, you make plans to do it.
*Mum and Dad **arranged** a trip to France.*
2 If you **arrange** things, you put them in order.
*Lisa **arranged** the books in neat piles.*

array arrays
An **array** is a group of things set out neatly in columns and rows.

arrive arrives, arriving, arrived
When you **arrive** at a place, you get there.

arrow arrows
1 An **arrow** is a thin stick with a point at one end and feathers at the other. It is shot from a bow.
2 An **arrow** is also a sign that points to something or shows you the way.

art
Art is paintings, drawings and sculptures.
*I saw lots of pictures at the **art** show.*

ask asks, asking, asked
1 You **ask** someone a question when you want to find the answer.
*"When is the party?" Simon **asked**.*
2 You **ask** for something when you want to be given it.
*"May I have some pudding?" Amy **asked**.*

asleep
When you are **asleep** your eyes are closed. You do not know what is happening around you.

assembly assemblies
An **assembly** is a group of people meeting together.
*We have school **assembly** every day.*

assistant assistants
An **assistant** is someone who helps another person.

astronaut astronauts
An **astronaut** flies in a spacecraft and travels in space.

ate See **eat**.

atlas atlases
An **atlas** is a book of maps.

attack attacks, attacking, attacked
If you **attack** someone, you try to harm them.

attention
When you watch and listen carefully, you are paying **attention**.

attract attracts, attracting, attracted
If something **attracts** you, you become interested in it.

audience audiences
The people who watch or listen to a concert, film or TV show are the **audience**.
*The **audience** laughed at the clowns.*

August
August is the eighth month of the year. It has 31 days.

aunt or auntie
aunts or aunties
Your **aunt** is the sister of your mother or father, or the wife of your uncle.

author authors
An **author** is a person who writes books or plays.

automatic
An **automatic** machine does things on its own.
*An **automatic** washing machine washes clothes on its own.*

autumn
Autumn is the season between summer and winter. It gets cooler and the leaves fall off many trees.

awake
When you are **awake**, your eyes are open. You know what is happening around you.

away
If you go **away**, you leave the place where you are.

awful
Awful means very bad.
*Dad had an **awful** cold.*

axe axes
An **axe** is a tool with a handle and a sharp metal edge. People chop wood with an **axe**.

baby babies
A **baby** is a very young child.

back backs
1 The **back** of something is the opposite side to the front.
2 Your **back** is the part of the body between your neck and your bottom.

backwards
1 If you walk **backwards**, you are walking in the direction that is behind you.
2 Backwards is the opposite way to forwards. If you say the alphabet **backwards**, you start at Z and finish at A.

bacon
Bacon is a kind of meat. It comes from a pig.
*We had eggs and **bacon** for breakfast.*

bad worse, worst
1 Something **bad** is not good.
2 Food is **bad** when it is too old to eat.

badge badges
A **badge** is a small sign with words and pictures. You wear it on your clothes.

badger badgers
A **badger** is a wild animal. It has black and white fur and lives underground. It comes out at night to hunt for food.

bag bags
A **bag** is used to hold things. It can be made of cloth, plastic, paper or leather.

bake bakes, baking, baked
When you **bake** food, you cook it in an oven.

baker bakers
A **baker** bakes and sells bread and cakes.

balance balances, balancing, balanced
1 When you **balance** something, you keep it steady and stop it from falling.
2 A **balance** is a weighing machine.
*Put these two parcels on the **balance** to see which one is heavier.*

ball balls

A **ball** is a round object. You can throw, catch, hit, roll or kick it.

ballet

Ballet is a special kind of dancing. It often tells a story.

balloon balloons

A **balloon** is a thin rubber bag. It can be blown up to make it float in the air.

banana bananas

A **banana** is a long fruit. You peel off its thick yellow skin to eat it.

band bands

1 A **band** is a group of people who play music together.
2 A **band** is also a narrow strip of something, such as a rubber band.

bandage bandages

A **bandage** is a strip of material. It is put over a cut to keep it clean.

bang bangs, banging, banged

1 A **bang** is a sudden loud noise.
*The balloon burst with a **bang**.*
2 When you **bang** something, you hit or shut it noisily.
*Harry **banged** the door shut.*

bank banks

1 People put their money in a **bank** to keep it safe.
2 A **bank** is also the land near the side of a river.

bar bars

1 A **bar** is a long piece of wood or metal.
2 A **bar** is also something made in a rectangular shape, like a **bar** of soap or a **bar** of chocolate.

bare

1 **Bare** means uncovered.
*Kim took her shoes off and danced in her **bare** feet.*
2 **Bare** can also mean empty.
*The fridge was **bare** so Mum bought some more food.*

bargain bargains

A **bargain** is something that is worth more than you pay for it.

bark barks, barking, barked

1 The **bark** of a tree is the hard part that covers its trunk.
2 A dog that **barks** makes a short, loud sound.

barn barns

A **barn** is a large building on a farm. Farmers store their crops in **barns**.

base

The **base** is the bottom part of something.
*The boys camped at the **base** of the mountain.*

a

Bb

c
d
e
f
g
h
i
j
k
l
m
n
o
p
q
r
s
t
u
v
w
x
y
z

basket   baskets
A **basket** is a container made of thin strips. It is used to store or carry things.

bat   bats
1 A **bat** is a piece of wood with a handle. It is used to hit a ball.
2 A **bat** is also an animal. It looks like a mouse with wings. **Bats** fly at night and hang upside down when they sleep.

bath   baths
A **bath** is a long container. You fill it with water and sit in it to wash your body.

bathroom   bathrooms
A **bathroom** is the room where you wash yourself.

battery   batteries
A **battery** is a small object that gives electricity. Watches and torches need the energy from **batteries** to work.

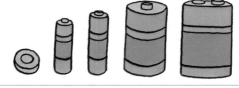

battle   battles
A **battle** is a fight between armies.

beach   beaches
A **beach** is the land at the edge of the sea. It is covered in sand or pebbles.

beak   beaks
A bird's **beak** is the hard part of its mouth.

bean   beans
A **bean** is a vegetable. There are different kinds, like red kidney **beans** and runner **beans**.

bear   bears
A **bear** is a large, wild furry animal with claws. Grizzly **bears** and polar **bears** are very big and heavy.

beard   beards
A **beard** is the hair that grows on a man's chin and cheeks.

beat   beats, beating, beat, beaten
1 When you **beat** someone in a race, you finish before they do.
2 If you **beat** something, you hit it again and again.
*The soldier was **beating** the drum.*

beautiful
Something that is lovely to see or hear is **beautiful**.
*The sunset was **beautiful** tonight.*

because

Because is a word used to give a reason why.
*We were late **because** we missed the bus.*

bed beds

A **bed** is a piece of furniture you sleep on.

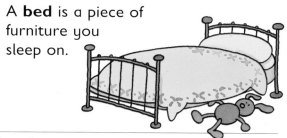

bedroom bedrooms

A **bedroom** is the room where you sleep. A **bedroom** has a bed in it.

bedtime

Bedtime is the time of day when you usually go to bed.

bee bees

A **bee** is an insect with wings. **Bees** make honey. Some **bees** live in beehives.

beetle beetles

A **beetle** is an insect. It has hard shiny wings.

before

If something is **before** something else, it happens earlier than it.
*I clean my teeth **before** I go to bed.*

begin begins, beginning, began, begun

You **begin** something when you start to do it.
*I always **begin** to get hungry at playtime.*

behave behaves, behaving, behaved

When you **behave** yourself, you are being good.

behind

If you are **behind** something, you are at the back of it.
*Lucy hid **behind** the fence.*

believe believes, believing, believed

When you **believe** something, you think it is true.

bell bells

A **bell** is something that rings when you hit, shake or press it.
*The school **bell** rings every morning.*

belong belongs, belonging, belonged

When something **belongs** to you, you own it.
*This bag **belongs** to me. It has my name on it.*

belt belts

A **belt** is a long strip of leather or cloth. It is worn around the waist.

bend bends, bending, bent

1 If you **bend** something, it is no longer straight.

2 A **bend** in a road is where it goes round a corner.

a

Bb

c

d

e

f

g

h

i

j

k

l

m

n

o

p

q

r

s

t

u

v

w

x

y

z

berry   **berries**

A **berry** is a small, juicy fruit that grows on bushes or trees.

best

If you are the **best**, you are better than anyone else at something.
*Pete was the **best** footballer ever.*
See **good** and **well**.

better

1 If you do something **better** than someone, they are not as good at it as you are.
*John is good at drawing, but Roberto is even **better**.*
2 If you have been ill, you are **better** when you feel well again.
See **good** and **well**.

between

1 Something that is **between** two other things is in the middle.
*The number 22 is **between** numbers 21 and 23.*
2 If you share something equally **between** two people, you give them the same amount or number.
*Jenny and Leela shared six sweets equally **between** them. They got three each.*

bicycle   **bicycles**

A **bicycle** is a vehicle with two wheels. You sit on it and turn the pedals with your feet.

big   **bigger, biggest**

Big means large in size.
*This is too **big** for me now. It will fit me when I'm bigger.*

bike   **bikes**

Bike is another word for bicycle.

bin   **bins**

A **bin** is a container. You put bread in a bread **bin** and rubbish in a rubbish **bin**.

bird   **birds**

A **bird** is an animal with feathers. It has two wings and two legs. Most **birds** can fly.

birthday   **birthdays**

Your **birthday** is the day you were born on.
*My **birthday** is on the first day of August.*

biscuit   **biscuits**

A **biscuit** is a kind of thin, hard cake.

bit   **bits**

1 *Sam **bit** the apple.*
See **bite**.
2 A **bit** is a very small piece of something.
*The cup smashed into **bits**.*

bite bites, biting, bit, bitten
When you **bite** something, you use your teeth to cut or tear it.
Sam is biting an apple.

blackberry blackberries
A **blackberry** is a small black fruit that grows on a bush.

blackbird blackbirds
A **blackbird** is a common bird. The male **blackbird** has black feathers and a yellow beak. The female is brown.

blackboard blackboards
A **blackboard** is used in a classroom. The teacher writes on it with chalk.

blade blades
A **blade** is the sharp part of a knife or an axe.

blame blames, blaming, blamed
1 If you **blame** someone, you say that they have done something wrong.
2 If you take the **blame**, you say that something was your fault.

blanket blankets
A **blanket** is a piece of thick cloth. It keeps you warm in bed.

blew See **blow**.

blind blinds
1 A **blind** person cannot see.
2 You pull a **blind** down over a window to keep out the light.

block blocks
A **block** is a solid piece of something.
Lizzie built a tower of wooden blocks.

block graph block graphs
A **block graph** is a kind of graph. The information is shown using blocks arranged in columns.

What we like to drink

number of children

juice milk tea water cola

blood
Blood is the red liquid that goes around inside your body.

blouse blouses
A **blouse** is a kind of shirt worn by girls and women. (See page 176.)

blow blows, blowing, blew, blown
1 You **blow** when you send air out through your mouth and nose.
Dad is blowing up the balloons for my party.

2 When the wind **blows**, the air moves faster.

a
Bb
c
d
e
f
g
h
i
j
k
l
m
n
o
p
q
r
s
t
u
v
w
x
y
z

19

blunt blunter, bluntest
When something is **blunt**, it is not sharp.

blurb
The **blurb** is the information about a book on its back cover.

boat boats
A **boat** is a vehicle that travels across water.

body bodies
A person's **body** is the whole of them.
*Your skin covers all your **body**.*

boil boils, boiling, boiled
1 Water **boils** when it gets very hot. You can see bubbles and steam.
2 When you **boil** food, you cook it in **boiling** water.

bold bolder, boldest
1 A **bold** person is brave. They are not afraid to do dangerous things.
2 Bold letters are dark and heavy, like the word **bold** in this sentence.

bomb bombs
A **bomb** is a weapon. It blows things apart.

bone bones
Bones are the hard white parts inside your body. They all join together to make your skeleton.

bonfire bonfires
A **bonfire** is a large fire that is lit outside.

bonnet bonnets
1 The **bonnet** is part of a car. (See page 175.)
2 A **bonnet** is a kind of hat.

book books
A **book** has pages held together inside a cover. The pages show words or pictures.

boot boots
1 A **boot** is a kind of shoe. It covers your foot and part of your leg.
2 A **boot** is also part of a car. (See page 175.)

bored
When you are **bored,** you are not interested in what you are doing.
*Adam was **bored** because it was raining and there was nothing to do.*

boring
Something **boring** is dull and not interesting.

born
A baby is **born** when it comes out of its mother's body.

borrow borrows, borrowing, borrowed
When you **borrow** something, you use it and give it back.
*Anil **borrows** books from the library.*

both

Both means two, not just one.
*Keep **both** hands on the handlebars!*

bottle bottles

A **bottle** is a container for liquids.
It is made of glass
or plastic and is
narrow at the top.
*Dad bought two
bottles of cola
for the party.*

bottom bottoms

1 The lowest part of something is its
bottom.
*The ball rolled down to the **bottom** of
the hill.*
2 Your **bottom** is the part of your
body that you sit on.

bought See **buy**.

bounce bounces, bouncing, bounced

When something
bounces, it jumps
back from a
hard surface.

bow bows, bowing, bowed

1 (*sounds like* cow)
When you **bow**, you
bend over at the waist.
*Jess **bowed** to the audience.*

2 (*sounds like* no)
A **bow** is a kind of knot.

3 (*sounds like* no)
A **bow** is also a bent piece
of wood used for shooting arrows.

bowl bowls

A **bowl** is a deep dish. You can put
soup or breakfast cereal in a **bowl**.

box boxes

A **box** is a container with straight
sides. It sometimes has a lid.
*Liam's shoes came in a cardboard **box**.*

boy boys

A **boy** is a child who will be a man
when he grows up.

bracelet bracelets

A **bracelet** is a piece of jewellery
that you wear around your wrist.

brain brains

Your **brain** is inside your head and
controls your body. You think and
remember with your **brain**.

brake brakes

The **brakes** of a bicycle or car make
it slow down or stop. (See page 175.)

branch branches

The **branches** of
a tree grow out
from the trunk.

brave braver, bravest

A **brave** person faces danger or pain
without showing fear.

bread

Bread is a food. It is made from flour
and baked in an oven.
*Nick likes **bread** and peanut butter.*

break **breaks, breaking, broke, broken**

1 When something **breaks**, it falls into pieces.

When Mum dropped the plate, it broke into little pieces.

2 When a machine is **broken**, it does not work properly.

The TV is broken. I can't watch cartoons.

breakfast

Breakfast is the first meal of the day.

breathe **breathes, breathing, breathed**

When you **breathe**, you take air in through your mouth and nose and then let it out again.

brick **bricks**

A **brick** is a block made from clay. **Bricks** are used to build houses.

bride **brides**

A **bride** is a woman on her wedding day.

bridesmaid   bride   bridegroom

bridegroom **bridegrooms**

A **bridegroom** is a man on his wedding day.

bridesmaid **bridesmaids**

A **bridesmaid** is a girl who helps a bride on her wedding day.

bridge **bridges**

A **bridge** is built over a road, river or railway line so that people and vehicles can cross it.

bright **brighter, brightest**

Something **bright** shines strongly.

brilliant

1 A **brilliant** light or colour is very bright.
2 A **brilliant** person is very clever.
3 A **brilliant** film or book is very, very good.

bring **brings, bringing, brought**

If you **bring** someone or something to a place, you take them with you.

Molly is bringing her sister to my house.

broke   See **break**.

broken   See **break**.

broom **brooms**

A **broom** is a brush with a long handle. It is used for sweeping floors.

brother **brothers**

Your **brother** is a boy who has the same parents as you do.

brought See **bring**.

---

brush **brushes**
A **brush** has a handle with lots of stiff hairs joined to it. **Brushes** come in lots of shapes and sizes. You use a **hairbrush** to make your hair tidy. You use a **toothbrush** to clean your teeth. **Paintbrushes** are for painting.

---

bubble **bubbles**
I A **bubble** is a ball of air. It is surrounded by a thin layer of liquid.
*Look at Zina's lovely **bubbles**! She is using a soapy liquid.*

2 In a cartoon, what people say is written in **speech bubbles**.

---

bucket **buckets**
A **bucket** is a container with a handle. It is made from plastic or metal.
*Mai Ling filled her **bucket** with sand.*

---

bud **buds**
A **bud** is a young flower or leaf before it opens.
*In the spring, **buds** appear on the trees.*

---

build **builds, building, built**
You **build** something when you put all its different parts together.

building **buildings**
A **building** has walls and a roof. Houses and schools are **buildings**. See **build**.

---

built See **build**.

---

bulb **bulbs**
I The **bulb** of a plant like an onion or tulip is the round part that grows in the soil.
2 A **bulb** is also the glass part of an electric lamp. It gives out light.

---

bull **bulls**
Cows and **bulls** are large farm animals. A **bull** is the male animal.

---

bullet **bullets**
A **bullet** is a small piece of metal. It is fired from a gun.

---

bump **bumps, bumping, bumped**
I If you **bump** into something, you knock into it suddenly.
*Charlie **bumped** into the table and knocked over the lamp.*
2 A **bump** is a swelling or lump on your body.
*Rose had a **bump** on her head.*

---

bumper **bumpers**
A **bumper** is part of a car.
(See page 175.)

---

bunch **bunches**
A **bunch** is a group of things that are joined or held together.
*I gave my mum a **bunch** of flowers. Dad bought her a **bunch** of grapes.*

a

Bb

c d e f g h i j k l m n o p q r s t u v w x y z

bungalow bungalows

A **bungalow** is a house with no upstairs.

burger burgers

A **burger** is a flat, round piece of cooked meat in a bun.

burglar burglars

A **burglar** goes into a building to steal things.

buried See **bury**.

burn burns, burning, burned, burnt

1 If something **burns**, it is on fire.
2 When you **burn** something, you hurt it or damage it by fire or heat.
3 A **burn** is a mark or injury caused by fire or heat.

burst bursts, bursting, burst

1 When something **bursts**, it breaks suddenly.
*The balloon **burst** with a loud bang.*
2 When somebody **bursts** into something, they do it suddenly.
*The baby **burst** into tears.*

bury buries, burying, buried

If you **bury** something, you put it in a hole in the ground and cover it up.
*The dog **buried** the bone in the garden.*

bus buses

A **bus** is a large vehicle with lots of seats. It carries people from one place to another.

bush bushes

A **bush** is a large woody plant with lots of branches.

bus stop bus stops

Buses stop at a **bus stop** to let people get on or off.

busy busier, busiest

A **busy** person has a lot to do.

butcher butchers

A **butcher** cuts up meat and sells it.

butter

Butter is a yellow food made from milk. You spread it on bread.

butterfly butterflies

A **butterfly** is an insect. It has large white or coloured wings.

button buttons

A **button** is a small round object sewn onto your clothes. You push it through a buttonhole to do your clothes up.

buy buys, buying, bought

You **buy** something when you pay money to get it.
*I **bought** this book with my birthday money.*

buzz buzzes, buzzing, buzzed

If something **buzzes**, it makes a humming sound like a bee.

cabbage   cabbages

A **cabbage** is a vegetable with green or purple leaves.

cable   cables

1 A **cable** is a bundle of wires covered in rubber which carries electricity.
2 Cable television reaches people's homes through underground wires.

café   cafés

You go to a **café** to have a snack or a drink.

cage   cages

A **cage** is a box or room with bars. Birds and animals are sometimes kept in **cages**.

cake   cakes

Cake is a sweet food. It is made by baking a mixture of flour, eggs, sugar and fat.

calculate   calculates, calculating, calculated

If you **calculate** something, you work it out.
Calculate the answer to 8 + 3 + 4.

calculation   calculations

A **calculation** is what you do when you work something out in maths. *Can you do this **calculation** in your head?*

calculator   calculators

A **calculator** is a small machine for doing calculations.

calendar   calendars

A **calendar** is a list that shows the days, weeks and months of the year. *I marked my birthday on the **calendar**.*

calf   calves

1 A **calf** is a young cow or bull.
2 Your **calf** is also the back of your leg, between your knee and your heel. (See page 174.)

call   calls, calling, called

1 If you **call** a person something, you give them a name.
2 If you **call** someone or give them a **call**, you telephone them.
3 If you **call** out, you speak loudly, sometimes with pain or excitement.
4 If you **call** on someone, you go to see them.

a b **Cc** d e f g h i j k l m n o p q r s t u v w x y z

a
b
Cc
d
e
f
g
h
i
j
k
l
m
n
o
p
q
r
s
t
u
v
w
x
y
z

calves See **calf**.

came See **come**.

camel **camels**
A **camel** is an animal that has one or two large humps on its back. **Camels** live in deserts and can travel a long way without water.

camera **cameras**
A **camera** is a machine that takes photographs, or film or television pictures.

camp **camps, camping, camped**
1 A **camp** is a group of tents or huts where people live or stay.
2 When you go **camping**, you live in a tent for a short time.

can **could; cans**
1 If you **can** do something, you are able to do it.
Peter can touch his toes.
2 A **can** is a metal container for liquids and food.
Mum opened a can of beans.

canal **canals**
A **canal** is a strip of water for boats to travel on. **Canals** are made by people.

candle **candles**
A **candle** is a stick of wax with string through the middle. You burn a **candle** to give you light.

cannot
If you **cannot** do something, you are not able to do it.
Paul cannot touch his toes.

can't
Can't is short for cannot.

cap **caps**
A **cap** is a small hat. It has a stiff piece sticking out at the front.

capacity
The **capacity** of something is the amount that it can hold.

capital **capitals**
1 A **capital** letter is a letter used at the beginning of a sentence or a name. **Capital** letters are sometimes called upper-case letters.
A B C D are capital letters and a b c d are lower-case letters.
2 A country's **capital** is the city from which it is controlled.
The capital of Italy is Rome.

captain **captains**
1 The leader of a group or team is often called the **captain**.
Rosie was captain of the rounders team.
2 A **captain** is also the person in charge of a ship or an aeroplane.

caption **captions**
A **caption** is the writing under a picture.

car cars

A **car** is a vehicle with four wheels and an engine. It can carry four or five people. (See page 175.)

caravan caravans

A **caravan** is a small house on wheels. It is pulled by a car or lorry.

card cards

1 A **card** is a piece of stiff paper with pictures and words on it. You send **cards** to people at special times like birthdays or when they are ill.
2 Playing **cards** have pictures or numbers on them. They are used to play games.

cardboard

Cardboard is very thick, stiff paper. It is used for making boxes.

care cares, caring, cared

1 If you **care** about something, it is important to you.
2 If you **care** for something, you look after it.
It's Peshpa's turn to care for the hamster.

careful

When you are **careful**, you think about what you are doing. You try not to make mistakes.

careless

When you are **careless**, you do not think about what you are doing. You often make mistakes.

carpet carpets

A **carpet** covers floors and stairs. It is usually made from wool.

carriage carriages

1 A **carriage** is a vehicle that carries people. It is pulled by horses.

2 A **carriage** is also the part of a train where passengers sit.

carrot carrots

A **carrot** is a long, orange vegetable. It grows under the ground.

carry carries, carrying, carried

If you **carry** something, you hold it and take it somewhere.

cartoon cartoons

1 In a **cartoon** film, all the pictures are drawn.
2 A **cartoon** is also a drawing that makes you laugh.

case cases

A **case** is a container to carry or keep things in.
I packed my case with clothes for my holiday.

a
b
Cc
d
e
f
g
h
i
j
k
l
m
n
o
p
q
r
s
t
u
v
w
x
y
z

a
b
Cc
d
e
f
g
h
i
j
k
l
m
n
o
p
q
r
s
t
u
v
w
x
y
z

castle **castles**

A **castle** is an old stone building. It has thick, high walls to protect the people inside.

cat **cats**

A **cat** is an animal with soft fur and sharp claws. Small **cats** are kept as pets. Lions and tigers are large **cats** that live in the wild.

catch **catches, catching, caught**

1 If you **catch** something that is moving, you stop it and hold it.
2 If you **catch** an illness, you become ill with it.
3 When you **catch** a bus, you get on it.

caterpillar **caterpillars**

A **caterpillar** is a creature that looks like a worm with legs. It becomes a butterfly or a moth.

cattle

Cows and bulls kept on a farm are **cattle**. Meat called beef and milk come from **cattle**.

caught See **catch**.

cauliflower **cauliflowers**

A **cauliflower** is a vegetable. It has a hard white centre and green leaves around the outside.

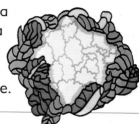

cave **caves**

A **cave** is a hollow place in the side of a mountain or underground.

CD **CDs**

A **CD** or compact disc is a flat plastic disc. It stores music, or information for use by a computer.

ceiling **ceilings**

A **ceiling** is the flat surface that covers the top of a room.

centimetre **centimetres**

Length, height, width or distance are measured in **centimetres**. There are 100 **centimetres** (cm) in a metre.

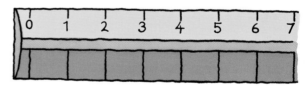

centre **centres**

1 The **centre** is the middle point of anything.
2 A **centre** is a place where people go for a special reason, like a health **centre**.

century **centuries**

A **century** is one hundred years.

cereal **cereals**

Breakfast **cereals** are foods eaten with milk. They are made from the seeds of oats, wheat or corn.

chain chains

A **chain** is a row of rings joined together in a line. **Chains** are usually made of metal.

chair chairs

A **chair** is a seat for one person. It has a back and sometimes has arms.

chalk

Chalk is a kind of soft white rock. Sticks of **chalk** are used for writing on a blackboard.

champion champions

A **champion** is someone who has won a competition.
*At the Olympics, the **champions** win gold medals.*

change changes, changing, changed

1 If you **change** something, you make it different.
2 When you get **changed**, you put on different clothes.
3 If you give too much money to pay for something, you are given **change**.
*I gave the shopkeeper too much money so he gave me some **change**.*

channel channels

1 A **channel** is a radio or television station.
*I switched over to **Channel** 2.*
2 A **channel** is also a narrow stretch of water.

chapter chapters

A **chapter** is a part of a book.
*Open your books at **Chapter** 3.*

character characters

A **character** is a person in a story, play or film.

charge charges, charging, charged

1 If someone **charges** you for something, they ask you to pay for it.
2 If you **charge**, you run forward, often to attack someone.
*The angry elephant **charged** through the forest.*
3 The person in **charge** of something is in control of it.
*Miss Dent is in **charge** of the class.*

chase chases, chasing, chased

If you **chase** someone, you run after them.

cheap cheaper, cheapest

Something **cheap** does not cost very much.

check checks, checking, checked

If you **check** something, you look at it carefully to see if it is all right.

checkout checkouts

A **checkout** is the place in a supermarket where you pay for your shopping.

cheek cheeks

Your **cheeks** are the soft parts on both sides of your face.
(See page 174.)

a
b
Cc
d
e
f
g
h
i
j
k
l
m
n
o
p
q
r
s
t
u
v
w
x
y
z

a
b
Cc
d
e
f
g
h
i
j
k
l
m
n
o
p
q
r
s
t
u
v
w
x
y
z

cheese cheeses

Cheese is a hard or soft food made from milk.

chemist chemists

A **chemist** is a person who sells medicines.

cherry cherries

A **cherry** is a small round fruit with a stone in the middle. **Cherries** can be red, yellow or black.

chest chests

I Your **chest** is the front part of your body between your neck and your tummy. (See page 174.)
2 A **chest** is a strong box with a lid.

chew chews, chewing, chewed

When you **chew** something, you keep biting it with your teeth to break it up.
Chew your food well before you swallow it.

chick chicks

A **chick** is a baby bird.

chicken chickens

A **chicken** is a large bird kept by farmers. **Chickens** give us eggs and meat.

chickenpox

Chickenpox is an illness. You get a fever and red spots on your skin.

chief chiefs

A **chief** is the leader of a group of people.

child children

A **child** is a young boy or girl.
*The **children** are playing on the swings.*

chimney chimneys

A **chimney** is an opening in a roof above a fire. Smoke goes up through the **chimney** into the air.

chimpanzee chimpanzees

A **chimpanzee** is a type of African ape. **Chimpanzees** are smaller than gorillas.

chin chins

Your **chin** is the bottom part of your face, below your mouth. (See page 174.)

chip chips

I A **chip** is a long piece of potato fried in oil.
2 If a cup has a **chip** in it, there is a small piece missing.
3 A **chip** is also a very small piece of metal that makes a computer work.

chocolate chocolates

Chocolate is a sweet, brown food that often comes in a bar. Drinks, cakes and puddings can taste of **chocolate**, too.

choose chooses, choosing, chose, chosen

If you **choose** something, you decide which one you want.
*I've **chosen** the biggest cake!*

chop chops, chopping, chopped

When you **chop** something, you cut it with a knife or axe.

chose See **choose**.

chosen See **choose**.

Christmas

Christmas is the 25th of December, when people celebrate Jesus Christ's birth. People often decorate a **Christmas** tree and give each other presents.

church churches

A **church** is a building where some people go to pray.

cinema cinemas

A **cinema** is a building where films are shown.

circle circles

A **circle** is a perfect round flat shape. The letter O is a **circle**.

circular

Anything in the shape of a circle is **circular**.

circus circuses

A **circus** is a travelling show. It is held in a large tent. You see clowns at a **circus**.

city cities

A **city** is a very large place where lots of people live. **Cities** are bigger than towns.

clap claps, clapping, clapped

When you **clap**, you make a noise by hitting your hands together.
*The children **clapped** to show they enjoyed Ravi's story.*

class classes

A **class** is a group of people who learn together.

classroom classrooms

A class has its lessons in a **classroom**.

claw claws

A **claw** is the sharp curved nail of an animal.
*The cat dug its **claws** into the sofa.*

a
b
Cc
d
e
f
g
h
i
j
k
l
m
n
o
p
q
r
s
t
u
v
w
x
y
z

a
b
Cc
d
e
f
g
h
i
j
k
l
m
n
o
p
q
r
s
t
u
v
w
x
y
z

clay
Clay is a kind of earth that is used to make bricks and pots.

clean cleans, cleaning, cleaned; cleaner, cleanest
1 You **clean** something to get the dirt off it.
2 Something that is **clean** has no dirty marks on it.

clear clearer, clearest
1 Something **clear** is easy to see through, like glass.
2 When something is **clear**, it is easy to see, hear or understand.
*This book has nice **clear** pictures.*
3 If something is **clear**, nothing covers it or gets in the way.
*The road was **clear** of snow.*

clever cleverer, cleverest
A **clever** person can do things easily and quickly.

cliff cliffs
A **cliff** is a hill with a steep side that goes straight down. **Cliffs** are usually near the sea.

climb climbs, climbing, climbed
You **climb** when you go up or down something high.
*My sister Lin **climbed** to the very top of the tree.*

clinic clinics
People go to a **clinic** for help when they are not well.
Ben's eye hurt, so he went to the eye clinic.

cloak cloaks
A **cloak** is a coat that has no sleeves.

clock clocks
A **clock** is a machine that tells you the time.

clockwise
If you go **clockwise**, you move in the same direction as the hands of a clock.

close closes, closing, closed; closer, closest
1 (*sounds like* nose) When you **close** something, you shut it.
2 (*sounds like* dose) **Close** means near.

closed
Closed means shut.

cloth cloths
1 **Cloth** is a soft material like cotton or wool. Your clothes are made of **cloth**.
2 A **cloth** is used to clean or cover things.

clothes

You wear **clothes** to keep you warm and dry. Jumpers and trousers are **clothes**. (See pages 176–177.)
When I get up, I put on my school clothes.

cloud clouds

You can see white or grey **clouds** floating in the sky. **Clouds** are made of very small drops of water which sometimes fall as rain.

clown clowns

A **clown** does silly things to make people laugh. **Clowns** have painted faces and wear funny clothes.

club clubs

A **club** is a group of people who meet often to do the same thing.
Jane and Tom go to the swimming club every Friday.

clue clues

A **clue** helps you to solve a problem or a mystery.

coach coaches

1 A **coach** is a bus used for long journeys.
2 A **coach** is also someone who helps you get better at a sport or lesson.
3 A **coach** can also be a kind of carriage.

coal

Coal is a black rock that is dug out of the ground. You can burn **coal** to get heat.

coast

The **coast** is the edge of the land where it meets the sea.

coat coats

You wear a **coat** over your other clothes when you go outside.

cobweb cobwebs

A **cobweb** is a thin net made by a spider. It catches flies and other insects.

cocoa

1 **Cocoa** is a brown powder used to make chocolate. It is made from the seeds of a tree.
2 **Cocoa** is also a hot drink that tastes of chocolate.

coconut coconuts

A **coconut** is a large nut with a hard hairy shell. Inside there is hard white flesh that you can eat and milky juice that you can drink.

cocoon cocoons

A **cocoon** is a small ball that a caterpillar spins. A caterpillar lives inside a **cocoon** as it changes into a butterfly or moth.

a
b
Cc
d
e
f
g
h
i
j
k
l
m
n
o
p
q
r
s
t
u
v
w
x
y
z

a
b
Cc
d
e
f
g
h
i
j
k
l
m
n
o
p
q
r
s
t
u
v
w
x
y
z

coffee

Coffee is a hot drink. You make it by pouring hot water onto a powder made from **coffee** beans.

coin coins

A **coin** is a piece of metal money.

cold colder, coldest; colds

1 When you are **cold**, you want to put on more clothes.
My feet are as cold as ice!
2 If you catch a **cold**, you feel ill and your nose runs.
Mum has a bad cold and can't stop sneezing.

collar collars

1 The **collar** of a shirt or coat is the part around the neck. It often folds over. (See page 177.)
2 A **collar** is also the band you put round the neck of a dog or cat.
My dog Lottie has her name and address on her collar.

collect collects, collecting, collected

1 If you **collect** something, you go and fetch it.
My dad collected the parcel from the post office.
2 When you put special things of the same kind together, you **collect** them.
I collect coins from all over the world.

colour colours

Red, yellow and blue are all **colours**. You can mix them together to get other **colours**. (See page 184.)
Green is the colour you get when you mix yellow and blue.

column columns

1 A **column** is a tall, solid cylinder.
The building had lots of columns.

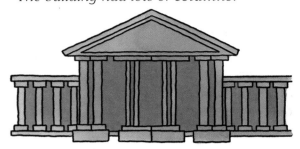

2 A **column** is a list of numbers or words. They go down a page one below the other.
The letters of the alphabet at the side of this page are in a column.

comb combs

A **comb** is a piece of plastic or metal with teeth. You use a **comb** to tidy your hair.

come comes, coming, came, come

1 When you **come** to a place, you arrive there.
When I came to school, the playground was nearly empty.
2 If someone asks you to **come**, they want you to go with them.

comfortable

Something **comfortable** feels nice to be in or to wear.
The chair was so comfortable that I fell asleep.

comic comics

A **comic** is a magazine for children. It tells stories in pictures.

a
b

Cc

d
e
f
g
h
i
j
k
l
m
n
o
p
q
r
s
t
u
v
w
x
y
z

comma commas

The punctuation mark , is a **comma**. It is used to make you stop very briefly when reading, like this, or in lists of things.

Nancy likes apples, oranges, pears and cherries.

commas

common

If something is **common**, you often see it. The opposite of **common** is rare.

compact disc compact discs

A **compact disc** is a flat, round, plastic object. It has music or information stored on it. It is also called a CD.

compare compares, comparing, compared

When you **compare** two things, you see how they are the same or different.

competition competitions

A **competition** is a test of who is best at something.

complete completes, completing, completed

1 If you **complete** something, you finish it.

*We **completed** the jigsaw puzzle.*

2 If something is **complete**, there is nothing left out.

*Here is a **complete** list of the people in my class.*

computer computers

A **computer** is a machine that stores and finds information. It can also do calculations, play games and control other machines.

concert concerts

A **concert** is a musical show.
*Ania sang in the school **concert**.*

cone cones

A **cone** has a circular top or bottom. Its other end comes to a point.
*We love to eat ice cream **cones**!*

confused

If you feel **confused**, you are not sure what to think or do.

conjunction conjunctions

A **conjunction** is a word that joins two parts of a sentence together. The words *and*, *but* and *or* are all **conjunctions**.

*I like cricket **and** football, **but** I don't like swimming **or** basketball.*

conker conkers

A **conker** is a shiny brown nut. It comes from a horse chestnut tree. You thread the nuts on string to play **conkers**.

a
b
Cc
d
e
f
g
h
i
j
k
l
m
n
o
p
q
r
s
t
u
v
w
x
y
z

consonant consonants

A **consonant** is any letter of the alphabet except for a, e, i, o, or u.

contain contains, containing, contained

Something **contains** the things that are inside it.

*My lunch box **contains** two sandwiches and an apple.*

container containers

A **container** is anything that you keep things in.

contents

The **contents** of something are the things inside it. The **contents page** of a book tells you what information is inside.

continue continues, continuing, continued

If you **continue** to do something, you keep on doing it.

*Please **continue** reading until you get to the bottom of the page.*

control controls, controlling, controlled

If you **control** something, you make it do what you want it to.

cook cooks, cooking, cooked

If you **cook** food, you make it ready to eat. You can fry, boil, bake or microwave it.

cooker cookers

A **cooker** is a machine for cooking food.

cool cooler, coolest

If you feel **cool**, you feel almost cold.

*On a hot day it is **cool** under the trees.*

copy copies, copying, copied

1 If you **copy** something, you make something that is exactly like it.

Copy the drawing into your book.

2 A **copy** of something looks exactly the same as it does.

corn

Cereal crops like wheat and oats are called **corn**.

corner corners

A **corner** is where two edges, sides or lines meet.

*A square has four **corners**.*

*Dad waited for me at the **corner** of the street.*

correct

If your answer is **correct**, you have not made any mistakes.

corridor corridors

A **corridor** is a long, narrow passage that leads to other rooms.

cost costs, costing, cost

1 If something **costs** an amount of money, that is what you pay for it.

2 The **cost** of something is what you must pay for it.

costume costumes

You wear a **costume** when you are pretending to be someone or something else.

Tom wore a costume in the school play.

cot cots

A **cot** is a bed for a baby. It has high sides to stop the baby from falling out of it.

cottage cottages

A **cottage** is a small house in the country.

cotton

1 Cotton is cloth made from the soft white seeds of a plant.
2 Cotton is also thread used to sew things together.

Mum used white cotton to sew on my name tapes.

cough coughs, coughing, coughed

When you **cough**, you clear your throat with a sudden loud noise.

could

If you **could** do something, you are able to do it or you were able to do it.

Molly could read when she was five.
See **can**.

count counts, counting, counted

1 If you **count**, you say numbers in the right order.

You count up to 100 and I'll hide.
Count back from 5 to 2.
Count on from 5 to 9.

2 When you **count** a group of things, you work out how many there are.

counter counters

1 A **counter** is a small round object. It is used in games that are played on a board.
2 In a small shop, you are served and pay your money at the **counter**.

country countries

1 A **country** is a land with its own people, language and laws.

Australia and Spain are countries.

2 The **country** is the land away from towns. You see farms, fields, trees and rivers in the **country**.

couple couples

1 A **couple** is two things of the same kind.
2 A **couple** is also two people who are married or going out together.

That young couple are about to get married.

cousin cousins

Your **cousin** is the son or daughter of your aunt or uncle.

a
b
Cc
d
e
f
g
h
i
j
k
l
m
n
o
p
q
r
s
t
u
v
w
x
y
z

a
b
Cc
d
e
f
g
h
i
j
k
l
m
n
o
p
q
r
s
t
u
v
w
x
y
z

cover covers, covering, covered

1 If you **cover** something, you put something else on it.
Harry covered his face with his hands.

2 A **cover** is something you put over or on another thing.
The cushion has a red cover.

cow cows

A **cow** is a large farm animal. You drink the milk that comes from **cows**.

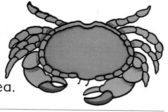

crab crabs

A **crab** is an animal with a hard shell. It lives in the sea.

crack cracks, cracking, cracked

1 If you **crack** a plate, thin lines appear on it but it does not break.
2 A **crack** is the thin line on something that is **cracked**.
3 A **crack** is also a loud noise.

cracker crackers

1 A **cracker** is a paper tube that bangs when it is pulled apart. It often has a paper hat and a toy inside.
2 A **cracker** is also a thin biscuit.

crane cranes

1 A **crane** is a tall machine for lifting heavy objects.
2 A **crane** is a tall bird with a long neck and legs. It lives near water.

crash crashes, crashing, crashed

1 When something **crashes**, it hits something else suddenly and noisily.
2 A **crash** is the noise of something **crashing**.
I heard the crash of breaking glass.
3 When a computer **crashes**, it suddenly stops working.

crawl crawls, crawling, crawled

When you **crawl**, you move along on your hands and knees.
The baby crawled across the floor.

crayon crayons

A **crayon** is used for drawing in colour. **Crayons** can be coloured pencils or made of wax.

cream

Cream is the thick liquid from the top of milk.
We had strawberries and cream for tea.

creature creatures

A **creature** is any animal.

creep creeps, creeping, crept

If you **creep**, you move slowly and quietly.
I tried to creep silently up the stairs.

cricket

Cricket is a game played with a bat and a ball. There are two teams of eleven players.

cried See **cry**.

cries See **cry**.

crisp crisps; crisper, crispest
1 A **crisp** is a thin slice of dry, fried potato. It is eaten cold.
Alan passed around a packet of crisps.
2 **Crisp** food is firm and breaks easily.
This lettuce is nice and crisp.

crocodile crocodiles
A **crocodile** is a large reptile with strong teeth. It is similar to an alligator.

crop crops
A **crop** is something that farmers grow to sell.

cross crosses, crossing, crossed; crosser, crossest
1 When you **cross** something, you go to the other side of it.
2 A little mark like x or + is a **cross**.
3 A **cross** person is angry.

crowd crowds
A **crowd** is a lot of people in one place.

crown crowns
A **crown** is a ring of gold and jewels. Kings and queens wear **crowns** on their heads.

cruel crueller, cruellest
A **cruel** person enjoys hurting others.

crumb crumbs
A **crumb** is a tiny piece of bread or cake.

crunch crunches, crunching, crunched
If you **crunch** food, you break it up noisily between your teeth.

cry cries, crying, cried
1 When you **cry**, tears fall from your eyes.
2 If you **cry** out, you shout.
3 A **cry** is a shout.

cub cubs
A **cub** is a young wild animal such as a tiger, fox or bear.

cube cubes
A **cube** is a shape with six square faces that are all the same size. Sugar is sometimes made into **cubes**.

cucumber cucumbers
A **cucumber** is a long, thin vegetable with dark green skin.

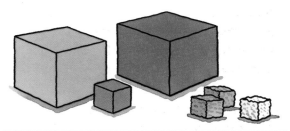

a
b
Cc
d
e
f
g
h
i
j
k
l
m
n
o
p
q
r
s
t
u
v
w
x
y
z

cuddle cuddles, cuddling, cuddled

When you **cuddle** someone, you put your arms around them.
Dad cuddled the baby.

cup cups

1 A **cup** is a small round container with a handle. You drink tea or coffee from a **cup**.
2 You can also win a **cup** as a prize. This kind of **cup** is made of metal.

cupboard cupboards

A **cupboard** is a piece of furniture with a door. You keep things in it.

curl curls, curling, curled

1 A **curl** is a piece of curved hair.
2 When you **curl** up, you bend your body into a little ball.

curly curlier, curliest

If you have **curly** hair, the pieces of hair make curls or rings.
Lindsay has long curly hair.

curry curries

Curry is food cooked with different spices.
The vegetable curry was hot and spicy.

curtain curtains

A **curtain** is a piece of cloth that hangs by a window. You can pull it across to keep out the light.

curved

If a line, road or surface bends, it is **curved**.

cushion cushions

A **cushion** is a bag filled with something soft. It is comfortable to lean against or sit on.

customer customers

A **customer** is someone who buys something in a shop.

cut cuts, cutting, cut

1 When you divide something with a sharp blade, you **cut** it.
Angus cut his birthday cake.
Mum cut my dad's hair.
2 If you **cut** yourself, you break open your skin and make it bleed.
3 A **cut** is an opening or wound made by something sharp.

cylinder cylinders

A **cylinder** is a tube with circular ends. It can be solid or hollow.

Dd

dad or **daddy** dads or daddies
Dad or **daddy** is what you call your father.

damage damages, damaging, damaged
When you **damage** something, you spoil it.
The cat scratched the chair and damaged it.

damp damper, dampest
If something is **damp**, it is a bit wet.
I've been drying my hair, but it still feels damp.

dance dances, dancing, danced
If you **dance**, you move in time to music.

danger dangers
If there is **danger**, something bad could happen.
Danger – thin ice!

dangerous
Something **dangerous** can hurt you.

dark darker, darkest
1 When it is **dark**, there is very little light or no light at all.
2 **Dark** hair is brown or black.

date dates
A **date** is the day, month and sometimes the year when something happens.
*Today's **date** is the 18th of September.*

daughter daughters
A person's **daughter** is their female child.

dawn
Dawn is the early morning, when it starts to get light.
*We got up at **dawn** to go fishing.*

day days
A **day** is made up of 24 hours. There are seven **days** in a week.

dead
If someone or something is **dead**, they are no longer alive.

deaf
A **deaf** person cannot hear well. Some **deaf** people cannot hear at all.

dear dearer, dearest
1 When you write a letter, you put **Dear** before the person's name.
2 Something **dear** is expensive.

a
b
c
Dd
e
f
g
h
i
j
k
l
m
n
o
p
q
r
s
t
u
v
w
x
y
z

December

December is the twelfth month of the year. It has 31 days.

decide decides, deciding, decided

You **decide** when you choose between two or more things.

deck decks

A **deck** is one of the floors of a ship or bus.
*Tom sat on the top **deck** of the bus.*

decorate decorates, decorating, decorated

1 If you **decorate** something, you make it look nice.
*Mum and I **decorated** the cake with icing.*
2 If you **decorate** a room, you paint it or paper the walls.

deep deeper, deepest

When something is **deep**, it is a long way down to its bottom.
*Be careful! The water is very **deep** here.*

deer deer

A **deer** is a large wild animal. The male **deer** may have horns called antlers.

defend defends, defending, defended

If you **defend** something, you protect it.

definition definitions

A **definition** tells you the meaning of a word. You find **definitions** in a dictionary.
*The **definition** of "baby" is "a very young child".*

delete deletes, deleting, deleted

If you **delete** something, you cross it out or remove it.

delicious

Food that is **delicious** smells and tastes lovely.

delighted

If you are **delighted**, you are very pleased.
*Mum was **delighted** when I won the race.*

deliver delivers, delivering, delivered

When you **deliver** something to someone, you take it to them.
*The postman **delivered** the parcel to our house.*

den dens

1 A **den** is the home of some wild animals. Bears, foxes and lions live in **dens**.
2 A **den** is also a secret place where children meet.

dentist dentists
A **dentist** looks after people's teeth.

depth
The **depth** of something is how deep it is.

describe describes, describing, described
When you **describe** something, you say what it is like.

description descriptions
The words that tell you about something are its **description**.
Sonia gave a description of the burglar to the police.

desert deserts
A **desert** is a hot, dry place. There is so little water that almost nothing grows.

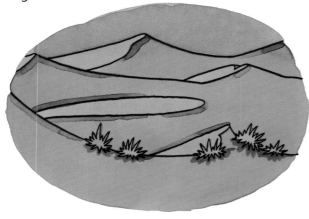

desk desks
A **desk** is a special table for working on. It sometimes has drawers to keep things in.

dessert desserts
A **dessert** is fruit or a sweet food served at the end of a meal. It can also be called a pudding.

destroy destroys, destroying, destroyed
If you **destroy** something, you damage it so much that it can never be used again.
The car was destroyed by fire.

diagram diagrams
A **diagram** is a drawing. It shows or explains how something works.

diamond diamonds
A **diamond** is a hard bright jewel. It looks like clear glass.
My granny has a ring with a diamond in it.

diary diaries
A **diary** is a book with a space for every day in the year. You write what happens in it.

dice
Dice are small cubes with numbers or spots on each face, usually from one to six.

dictionary dictionaries
A **dictionary** is a book that lists words in alphabetical order. It tells you how to spell them and what they mean.

did See **do**.

didn't
Didn't is short for did not.

die dies, dying, died
When people, animals and plants **die**, they stop living.

difference differences
1 A **difference** between two things is what is not the same about them.
2 The **difference** between two numbers is the answer you get when you take the smaller number away from the larger number.
*The **difference** between 5 and 3 is 2.*

different
1 When two or more things are **different**, they are not the same.
2 If something is **different**, it has changed in some way.
*Your hair looks **different** – have you had it cut?*

difficult
Something **difficult** is hard to do or to understand.
*These puzzles are very **difficult**.*

dig digs, digging, dug
When you **dig** soil or sand, you use your hands or a spade to pick it up and move it.

digit digits
A **digit** is a symbol used to write numbers. There are ten different **digits** in our number system: 0, 1, 2, 3, 4, 5, 6, 7, 8 and 9.
*In the number 47, the **digits** are 4 and 7. 47 is a two-**digit** number.*

digital
A **digital** watch or clock has no hands. It gives the time in numbers.

dinner dinners
Dinner is the main meal of the day. It is sometimes the evening meal. Some people call the midday meal **dinner**.

dinner time
Dinner time is the time of day when you usually eat your dinner.

dinosaur dinosaurs
Dinosaurs were huge animals that lived on Earth 65 million years ago.
(See pages 172–173.)

dip dips, dipping, dipped
When you **dip** something, you put it in liquid briefly.
*Mary **dipped** her toe in the water.*

direction directions
1 If you are moving in a certain **direction**, that is the way you are going.
2 **Directions** are instructions about how to get somewhere.

dirt
Dirt is anything that makes things not clean, such as dust or mud.

dirty dirtier, dirtiest
Something **dirty** has dirt on it.
*My shoes were **dirty** after playtime.*

disappear disappears, disappearing, disappeared
If something **disappears**, it suddenly goes out of sight.
*The car **disappeared** around the corner.*

disappointed
You are **disappointed** when something that happens is not as good as you hoped.
*I was very **disappointed** when our team lost the match.*

disaster disasters
A **disaster** is something very bad that happens, causing damage and death. An air crash or an earthquake is a **disaster**.

disc discs
A **disc** is a flat circular piece of anything.

discover discovers, discovering, discovered
If you **discover** something, you find out about it or see it for the first time.

discuss discusses, discussing, discussed
You **discuss** something when you talk about it with other people.

disguise disguises
You wear a **disguise** so that people will not know who you are.
*Is that Hamish wearing a **disguise**?*

dish dishes
A **dish** is a plate or bowl for food.

dishwasher dishwashers
A **dishwasher** is a machine that washes dirty plates, cups and saucepans.

disk disks
Disk is another way of spelling disc.

distance distances
The **distance** between two things is how far it is between them.
*The **distance** between Richard and Caroline is about 3 metres.*

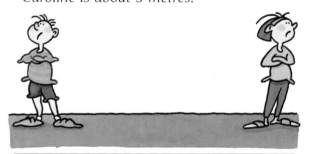

disturb disturbs, disturbing, disturbed
When you **disturb** someone, you stop them doing what they are doing.
*Please don't **disturb** me – I'm trying to read.*

dive dives, diving, dived
If you **dive**, you jump head first into water. You hold your arms straight above your head.
*Sadiya **dived** off the top board.*

a b c **Dd** e f g h i j k l m n o p q r s t u v w x y z

divide divides, dividing, divided

If you **divide** something, you share it into equal groups.

*You can **divide** 6 sweets into 3 groups of 2.*

$6 \div 3 = 2$

division divisions

Division is what you do when you divide numbers or things.

Diwali

Diwali is a Hindu festival. It is also called the festival of light.

do does, doing, did, done

When you **do** something, you carry out an activity.

*Emma is **doing** her homework.*

doctor doctors

A **doctor** looks after people's health.

does See **do**.

doesn't

Doesn't is short for does not.

dog dogs

A **dog** is an animal that barks. **Dogs** are often kept as pets.

doll dolls

A **doll** is a toy that looks like a baby or small person.

dolphin dolphins

A **dolphin** is a mammal that lives in the sea. It looks like a fish with a large nose.

domino dominoes

A **domino** is a flat rectangular block used for playing a game. It has up to six spots on each half.

done See **do**.

donkey donkeys

A **donkey** is an animal rather like a small horse. It has long ears.

don't

Don't is short for do not.

*I really **don't** like rice pudding!*

door doors

A **door** is a piece of wood, metal or glass that closes the way into a building, room or piece of furniture.

*Liam opened the front **door**.*

doorbell doorbells

A **doorbell** is a bell on the outside of a house. You ring it to tell the people inside that you are there.

dot dots

A **dot** is a very small round mark.

*You put a **dot** over the letter i.*

a b c **Dd** e f g h i j k l m n o p q r s t u v w x y z

double doubles, doubling, doubled

1 If you **double** something, you multiply it by two. You can also add two of the same numbers together.
6 × 2 and 6 + 6 are both ways of finding double 6.
2 If something is **double** the size, it is twice as big.

downstairs

If you go **downstairs**, you go down to a lower floor.
Let's go downstairs to play.

drag drags, dragging, dragged

When you **drag** something, you pull it along the ground.

dragon dragons

In stories, a **dragon** is a pretend animal with wings and claws. It can breathe out fire.

drain drains

A **drain** is a pipe to carry liquid like bath water away.

drank See **drink**.

draw draws, drawing, drew, drawn

1 When you **draw**, you make a picture using pencil, crayons or chalk. You can also **draw** on a computer screen using a mouse.
2 When a game ends in a **draw**, the two sides have the same score.

drawer drawers

A **drawer** is a box that slides in and out of a piece of furniture. You keep things in **drawers**.

drawing drawings

A **drawing** is a picture made with a pen or pencil.
See **draw**.

drawn See **draw**.

dream dreams, dreaming, dreamed or dreamt

When you **dream**, thoughts and pictures come into your mind while you are asleep.

dress dresses, dressing, dressed

1 When you **dress**, you put on your clothes.
2 A **dress** is a piece of clothing worn by a girl or woman. It covers her from her shoulders to her legs.

dressing gown dressing gowns

A **dressing gown** is a piece of clothing. It is like a coat and you wear it over your night clothes. (See page 176.)

drew See **draw**.

a
b
c
Dd
e
f
g
h
i
j
k
l
m
n
o
p
q
r
s
t
u
v
w
x
y
z

a
b
c

Dd

e
f
g
h
i
j
k
l
m
n
o
p
q
r
s
t
u
v
w
x
y
z

drink **drinks, drinking, drank, drunk**
1 When you **drink**, you put liquid into your mouth and swallow it.
2 A **drink** is a liquid that you swallow.
*Would you like a **drink** of milk?*

drip **drips, dripping, dripped**
When liquid **drips**, it falls in small drops.

drive **drives, driving, drove, driven**
1 When you **drive** a car, you make it go where you want it to.
2 A **drive** is a journey in a car.

drop **drops, dropping, dropped**
1 When you **drop** something, you let it fall.
*The dog **dropped** the stick.*
2 A **drop** is a very small amount of liquid.

drove See **drive**.

drown **drowns, drowning, drowned**
If someone **drowns**, they die under water because they cannot breathe.

drum **drums**
A **drum** is a musical instrument that you hit to make a sound.

drunk See **drink**.

dry **drier or dryer, driest**
Something **dry** has no liquid on it.

duck **ducks**
A **duck** is a bird that can swim and fly. It lives near water.

dug See **dig**.

dull **duller, dullest**
1 Dull means not clear or bright.
2 Dull also means boring.

dungeon **dungeons**
A **dungeon** is a dark, underground prison beneath a castle.

dusk
Dusk is the time just before it gets dark in the evening.

dust
Dust is a dry, fine powder. It is carried on the air.

dustbin **dustbins**
A **dustbin** is a large metal or plastic container for rubbish.

duvet **duvets**
A **duvet** is a large cloth bag filled with something soft. You sleep under it to keep warm.

dying See **die**.

each
Each means every one of a number of things or people.
*Give **each** child two pencils.*

eagle   eagles
An **eagle** is a large bird with a curved beak. It lives among mountains.

ear   ears
Your **ears** are on each side of your head. Your **ears** help you to hear. (See page 174.)

early   earlier, earliest
1 If you are **early**, you arrive before you are expected.
2 The **early** part of something is near the beginning.
*I play football in the **early** morning.*

earn   earns, earning, earned
You **earn** money by working for it.
*I **earned** some pocket money by washing the car.*

earring   earrings
An **earring** is a piece of jewellery that you wear on your ear.

earth
1 The planet **Earth** is the world we live on.

2 The soil that plants grow in is also called **earth**.

earthquake   earthquakes
When there is an **earthquake**, the ground shakes suddenly. Sometimes buildings fall down.

east
East is the direction you look in to see the sun rise.

Easter
Easter is a spring festival when Christians remember Jesus Christ coming back from the dead.

easy   easier, easiest
Something **easy** is simple to do or understand.
*The sums were much **easier** than I expected.*

eat   eats, eating, ate, eaten
When you **eat** something, you put it into your mouth and swallow it.
*I'm going to **eat** my apple at playtime.*

echo   echoes
You hear an **echo** when a sound that you make comes back to you.
*Anil shouted his name in the cave and heard the **echo**.*

edge edges

1 The **edge** of something is the part furthest from its centre.
My pillow fell off the edge of my bed.

2 An **edge** is where two faces of a solid object meet.
This box has 12 edges.

effort efforts

If you make an **effort**, you try very hard to do something.
Nick made a real effort to write well.

egg eggs

Baby birds, snakes, fish and insects hatch from **eggs**. Hens lay **eggs** that people can eat.

elastic

When you pull **elastic**, it stretches. When you let go, it goes back to its normal size.

elbow elbows

Your **elbow** is the middle part of your arm which bends.
(See page 174.)

electric

Something **electric** works by electricity.

electricity

Electricity is one kind of energy. It is used to give heat and light and to make machines work.

elephant elephants

An **elephant** is a very large land animal. It has a long nose called a trunk.

e-mail or email
e-mails or emails
An **e-mail** is a message that you send from one computer to another.

emerald emeralds
An **emerald** is a green jewel.

empty emptier, emptiest
If something is **empty**, there is nothing in it.

encyclopedia or encyclopaedia
encyclopedias or encyclopaedias
An **encyclopedia** is a book or CD with information on lots of different things.

end ends, ending, ended

1 The **end** of something is where it finishes.
We walked to the end of the street.
2 Something **ends** when it stops happening.
The film ends at eight o'clock.

ending endings
The **ending** is the last part of something.
The story had a sad ending.

enemy enemies

An **enemy** is someone who fights against you or your country.

energetic

An **energetic** person is full of life and always active.

energy

Energy is the power that makes things happen. People need **energy** to move and do things. Machines need **energy** to make them work. Electricity is one kind of **energy**.

engine engines

An **engine** is a machine that makes things like cars and trains move.

enjoy enjoys, enjoying, enjoyed

If you **enjoy** doing something, you like doing it and it makes you happy.

enormous

Enormous means very large.

enough

Something that is **enough** is as much as you need or want.
*Has Meena had **enough** to eat?*

enter enters, entering, entered

1 If you **enter** a place, you go into it.
2 If you **enter** something on a computer, you key it in.

entrance entrances

An **entrance** is the way into a place.

envelope envelopes

An **envelope** is a paper cover for a letter.

John Hardy
14 Victoria Road
Greentown

environment environments

The **environment** is the air, water and land around us.

equal equals, equalling, equalled

1 If two things are **equal**, they are the same size or number.
*One week is **equal** to seven days.*
2 Equals means that two numbers or quantities are the same.
The symbol = means **equals**.
$5 - 1 = 4$

equipment

Equipment is the set of things needed for something or to do something.
*Miss Jones got out the PE **equipment**.*

escape escapes, escaping, escaped

If you **escape** something, you get away from it.
*The animals **escaped** from the burning forest.*

estimate estimates, estimating, estimated

1 If you **estimate** the answer to something, you make a careful guess.
2 An **estimate** is a careful guess.

a
b
c
d
Ee
f
g
h
i
j
k
l
m
n
o
p
q
r
s
t
u
v
w
x
y
z

a
b
c
d
Ee
f
g
h
i
j
k
l
m
n
o
p
q
r
s
t
u
v
w
x
y
z

even
1 If a number is **even**, it can be divided exactly by two.
2 Even also means flat and smooth.

evening   evenings
Evening is the last part of the day. It starts to get dark and you go to bed.

ever
Ever means at any time.
*Have you **ever** been to France?*

every
Every means each one of a number of things or people.
*Give **every** girl a hat and **every** boy a cap.*

everybody
Everybody means every person.
*Has **everybody** given me their homework?*

everyone
Everyone is another word for everybody.

everything
Everything means all the things.
*Have you put **everything** away?*

everywhere
Everywhere means every place.
*The dog followed her **everywhere**.*

evil
An **evil** person is very bad.

exact
An **exact** answer cannot be any better or closer.

exactly
If you say a number or time **exactly**, it is not less or more than that.
*I cut the cake into **exactly** three pieces.*

example   examples
You use an **example** to show what you mean.
*Tom's picture is a good **example** of how to use paint.*

excellent
Something **excellent** is very good.
*Gill's work was **excellent**.*

except
Except means not including someone or something.
*Everyone got a sweet **except** me.*

exchange   exchanges, exchanging, exchanged
If you **exchange** something, you give it away and receive something else instead.
*I **exchanged** my book for a different one.*

excited

If you are **excited**, you are so happy that you want to jump about.
*I'm really **excited** about my birthday!*

exclaim exclaims, exclaiming, exclaimed

If you **exclaim**, you cry out suddenly.
*"Ouch! That hurt!" Dad **exclaimed**.*

exclamation mark
exclamation marks

A mark like ! is an **exclamation mark**. It is used to show that someone exclaims.
I can't wait until my birthday!

excuse excuses

An **excuse** is a reason you give for doing or not doing something.
*You're late. What is your **excuse**?*

exercise exercises

1 Exercise is anything active that you do to keep fit.

2 An **exercise** is a set of questions that help you practise something.
Practise your tables by doing Exercise 5 for homework.

exit exits

An **exit** is a way out of a place.
*The **exit** is blocked and I can't get out.*

expect expects, expecting, expected

If you **expect** something to happen, you believe it will happen.
*Dan's the fastest, so I **expect** him to win.*

expensive

Something **expensive** costs a lot.

explain explains, explaining, explained

If you **explain** something, you say what it means or why it happened.

explanation explanations

An **explanation** says what something means or why it happened.

explode explodes, exploding, exploded

When something **explodes**, it blows up into small pieces with a loud bang.

explore explores, exploring, explored

If you **explore** a place, you look around to see what it is like.

extinct

An animal that is **extinct** has died out. There will never be any more of them.
*Dinosaurs are **extinct**.*

extra

Something **extra** is more than usual.
*My mum gave me **extra** pocket money.*

eye eyes

Your **eyes** are parts of your face. You see with your **eyes**.
(See page 174.)

a
b
c
d
Ee
f
g
h
i
j
k
l
m
n
o
p
q
r
s
t
u
v
w
x
y
z

53

Ff

face   faces

1 Your **face** is the front of your head. (See page 174.)

2 A **face** of a solid object is any one of its surfaces.
A cube has six faces.

fact   facts

A **fact** is something that is true.
It is a fact that the Earth goes round the Sun.

factory   factories

Things are made in a **factory**, usually using machines.

fail   fails, failing, failed

You **fail** if you try to do something but cannot do it.
I tried to ring Anna, but I failed.

fair   fairer, fairest; fairs

1 A **fair** person treats everyone the same.

2 A person who is **fair** is beautiful.
*"Mirror, mirror, on the wall,
Who is the fairest of them all?"*

3 Someone with **fair** hair has pale hair.

4 A **fair** is an outdoor show that moves from town to town.
I went on an exciting ride at the fair.

fairy   fairies

In stories, a **fairy** is a very small person. **Fairies** have wings and magic powers.
Zina is dressed as a fairy.

fairy tale   fairy tales

A **fairy tale** is a story where magical things happen.

fall   falls, falling, fell, fallen

1 If something **falls**, it drops towards the ground.
The apples fell from the tree onto the grass.

2 If you **fall** asleep, you go to sleep.

false

Something is **false** when it is not true or is not real.
The clown wore a false nose.

family   families

Your parents, brothers, sisters, grandparents, aunts, uncles and cousins are your **family**.

famous

Someone **famous** is very well known.
Dick King-Smith is a famous writer.

fantastic

If you say something is **fantastic**, you mean that it is wonderful.

far   farther or further, farthest or furthest

Far means a long way.
Are you going far?

farm farms

A **farm** is a place in the country where a farmer grows food or keeps animals.

farmer farmers

A **farmer** lives on a farm. **Farmers** grow food and look after animals.

fast faster, fastest; fasts, fasting, fasted

1 Something **fast** moves very quickly.
2 If you **fast**, you do not eat any food.

fasten fastens, fastening, fastened

When you **fasten** something, you fix one thing firmly to another.
*Please **fasten** your seat belt.*

fat fatter, fattest

1 A **fat** person or animal has a round, heavy body.
*Our dog is **fat**. She can't fit into her kennel.*
2 **Fat** is a food. Butter is a kind of **fat**.

father fathers

A **father** is a man who has a son or daughter.

fault

It is your **fault** if you cause something bad to happen.
*It's John's **fault** the plant died, because he forgot to water it.*

favourite

Your **favourite** is the one you like best.
*Blue is my **favourite** colour.*

fax faxes

You use a **fax** to send a copy of a letter or picture to someone.

fear fears, fearing, feared

1 If you **fear** someone or something, they frighten you.
2 **Fear** is the nasty feeling you get when you are afraid.
*My mum has a **fear** of spiders.*

feast feasts

A **feast** is a large, special meal for lots of people.

feather feathers

Feathers cover the body of a bird. They are very light.

February

February is the second month of the year. It usually has 28 days. In a leap year, it has 29 days.

feed feeds, feeding, fed

When you **feed** a person or animal, you give them food.
*Did you **feed** the dog?*

feel feels, feeling, felt

1 When you **feel** happy, you are happy at that moment.
2 When you touch something to find out what it is like, you **feel** it.

feet See **foot**.

a
b
c
d
e

Ff

g
h
i
j
k
l
m
n
o
p
q
r
s
t
u
v
w
x
y
z

fell See **fall**.

felt See **feel**.

female females
A **female** person or animal can be a mother. Girls and women are **females**.

fence fences
A **fence** is a kind of wall around a garden or field. It is made from wood or wire.

ferry ferries
A **ferry** is a kind of boat. It carries people and vehicles across a river or a narrow piece of sea.

festival festivals
1 A **festival** is a number of special shows. A **festival** is often held every year.
2 A **festival** is also a special time, like Christmas or Diwali.
We all bring fruit and vegetables to school for our Harvest Festival.

fetch fetches, fetching, fetched
If you **fetch** something, you go and get it from another place.
I fetched my bike from the shop.

fete or fête fetes or fêtes
A **fete** is an outdoor show. There are competitions and things to eat and drink.
We went to the school fete on Saturday.

fever fevers
A **fever** is an illness that makes you very hot.

few fewer, fewest
Few means not many.
There are only a few seats left.

fiction
Fiction is stories that have been made up about people or animals that are not real.

field fields
A **field** is a piece of land on a farm. It has a fence or hedge around it.

fierce fiercer, fiercest
A **fierce** animal is very angry and likely to attack.
The fierce dog barked angrily.

fight fights, fighting, fought
When people or animals **fight**, they try to hurt each other.

figure figures
A **figure** is another word for a number or an amount.

fill fills, filling, filled
When you **fill** something, you use up the space inside it.
Mum filled my glass with orange juice.

film films

1 A **film** is a story shown on a screen using moving pictures.

2 You put a roll of **film** in your camera to take pictures.

fin fins

A **fin** is part of a fish. It helps the fish to travel through the water.

find finds, finding, found

1 When you see something that you are looking for, you **find** it.
2 When you **find** out about something, you learn something new. *Today we are going to **find** out about the weather.*

fine finer, finest

1 Something that is **fine** is very good. *A **fine** day is sunny and dry.*
2 **Fine** can also mean that something is very thin, like a line or a thread.

finger fingers

You have five **fingers** on each hand. (See page 174.)

finish finishes, finishing, finished

When you **finish** something, you come to the end of it, use it up or do the last part of it.

fire fires

1 **Fire** is the heat and light given off when things burn.
2 People have a **fire** to keep warm.

fire brigade fire brigades

A **fire brigade** is a group of firefighters. People call the **fire brigade** to put out a dangerous fire.

fire engine fire engines

A fire brigade travels in a **fire engine**.

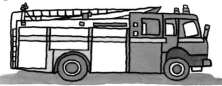

firefighter firefighters

A **firefighter** puts out dangerous fires.

firework fireworks

When someone lights a **firework**, it sends out bright, coloured lights.

firm firmer, firmest

Something that is **firm** does not move easily when you push it.

first

When someone or something is **first**, they come before all the others. *January is the **first** month of the year.*

fish fish or fishes

A **fish** is an animal that lives under water. **Fish** are covered with scales.

a
b
c
d
e
Ff
g
h
i
j
k
l
m
n
o
p
q
r
s
t
u
v
w
x
y
z

fisherman fishermen
A **fisherman** is someone who catches fish.

fit fits, fitting, fitted; fitter, fittest
1 If something **fits**, it is the right size and shape.
2 If you are **fit**, you feel healthy and well.

fix fixes, fixing, fixed
1 If you **fix** something that was broken, you mend it.
*Dad managed to **fix** his car.*
2 If you **fix** two things together, you join them to each other.

flag flags
A **flag** is a rectangle of cloth with a coloured pattern on it. It flies from a pole. Every country in the world has its own **flag**.

flame flames
A **flame** is a hot, bright tongue of fire.

flap flaps, flapping, flapped
Something that **flaps** is joined to something on one side and moves backwards and forwards.
*The bird **flapped** its wings.*

flash flashes
A **flash** is a short, sudden, bright light.
*A **flash** of lightning lit up the sky.*

flat flatter, flattest; flats
1 A **flat** surface has no bumps or slopes.
2 A **flat** is a home on one floor. It is part of a bigger building.

flavour flavours
The **flavour** of food or drink is what it tastes like.
*I love ice cream – chocolate is my favourite **flavour**.*

flew See **fly**.

flies See **fly**.

flip flips, flipping, flipped
If you **flip** something, you turn it quickly and suddenly.
*Nadia **flipped** over the page.*

float floats, floating, floated
1 Something that **floats** in a liquid does not sink. It stays on top.
*The plastic duck **floated** on the water.*

2 Something that **floats** through the air moves slowly without getting lower.
*The balloon **floated** across the sky.*

flock flocks
A **flock** is a group of birds, sheep or goats.
*A **flock** of birds flew overhead.*

flood floods

There is a **flood** when water covers an area that is usually dry.
Boats came to rescue people from the flood.

floor floors

1 The **floor** of a room is the part you walk on.
I have a blue carpet on my bedroom floor.
2 A **floor** is all the rooms on the same level in a building.
Gran's flat is on the sixth floor.

floppy disk floppy disks

A computer can store information on a **floppy disk**.

flour

Flour is a white or brown powder made from wheat. It is used to make bread and cakes.

flow flows, flowing, flowed

If a liquid **flows**, it moves from place to place.
A river flows through our town.

flower flowers

A **flower** is a part of a plant. It makes seeds. Some **flowers** have coloured petals.

fly flies, flying, flew, flown

1 If you **fly**, you travel through the air.
2 A **fly** is a small flying insect.

fog

Fog is thick cloud that is near the ground. It makes it difficult to see.

foggy

When it is **foggy**, it is difficult to see because of the fog.

fold folds, folding, folded

If you **fold** something, you bend it over on itself.
Susan folded up her towel.

follow follows, following, followed

If you **follow** someone, you move along behind them.
We all followed Emma to the hall.

food foods

Food is anything that people and animals eat to stay alive. **Food** gives you the energy to do things.
My favourite food is fish fingers.

foot feet

1 Your **foot** is at the end of your leg. (See page 174.)
2 A **foot** is an older way to measure length.

football footballs

Football is a game played by two teams. They try to kick a **football** into a goal. Another word for **football** is soccer.

a
b
c
d
e
Ff
g
h
i
j
k
l
m
n
o
p
q
r
s
t
u
v
w
x
y
z

a
b
c
d
e
Ff
g
h
i
j
k
l
m
n
o
p
q
r
s
t
u
v
w
x
y
z

footprint **footprints**
Footprints are the marks your feet leave when you walk in snow or wet sand.

forehead **foreheads**
Your **forehead** is the top of your face. (See page 174.)

foreign
Something that is **foreign** comes from another country.
*My family eats **foreign** food from all over the world.*

forest **forests**
A **forest** is a place where lots of trees grow together.

forgave   See **forgive**.

forget **forgets, forgetting, forgot, forgotten**
If you **forget** something, you do not remember it.
*I **forgot** it was Mum's birthday.*

forgive **forgives, forgiving, forgave, forgiven**
If you **forgive** someone, you stop being angry with them.
*Mum **forgave** me for breaking her watch.*

forgot   See **forget**.

forgotten   See **forget**.

fork **forks**
A **fork** is a tool with sharp points and a handle. You use a **fork** to help you eat your food.

fortnight **fortnights**
A **fortnight** is the same as two weeks.

forwards
1 If you walk **forwards**, you are going in the direction that is in front of you.
2 Forwards is the opposite way to backwards. If you say the alphabet **forwards**, you start at A and finish at Z.

fossil **fossils**
A **fossil** is a plant or animal that has turned to stone.
A **fossil** has been in the ground for many thousands of years.

fought   See **fight**.

found   See **find**.

fountain **fountains**
A **fountain** is a jet of water that shoots up into the air.

fox **foxes**
A **fox** is a wild animal that looks like a dog. It has a thick tail.

fraction fractions

A **fraction** is part of a whole number or shape. A half ($\frac{1}{2}$) and a quarter ($\frac{1}{4}$) are both **fractions**.

$\frac{1}{2}$ $\frac{1}{4}$

frame frames

A **frame** is the wood, metal or plastic around a picture or a window.

freckle freckles

Freckles are tiny brown spots on a person's skin.

free

1 If you are **free**, you can choose where you go and what you do.
2 Something that is **free** does not cost any money.
*The supermarket gave away **free** balloons.*

freeze freezes, freezing, froze, frozen

1 Water **freezes** when it gets very cold. It changes from water into ice.
2 If you are **freezing**, you are very, very cold.

fresh fresher, freshest

1 When something is **fresh**, it is new and clean.
*Turn to a **fresh** page.*
2 **Fresh** food is not old or bad.
3 **Fresh** water is not salty from the sea. It is rain water that has collected in a river or lake.

Friday Fridays

Friday is the day of the week between Thursday and Saturday.

fridge fridges

A **fridge** is a machine that keeps food cold and fresh. **Fridge** is short for refrigerator.

fried See **fry**.

friend friends

A **friend** is a person you know well and like very much.
*I play with my best **friend** every day.*

friendly friendlier, friendliest

A **friendly** person is kind and easy to get on with.

fries

Fries are thin chips.
See **fry**.

frighten frightens, frightening, frightened

1 If you **frighten** someone, you make them afraid.
2 If you are **frightened**, you feel afraid.
*My dog is **frightened** of loud noises.*

frog frogs

A **frog** is a small animal that can swim and jump. **Frogs** live on land and in water.

a b c d e **Ff** g h i j k l m n o p q r s t u v w x y z

a
b
c
d
e
Ff
g
h
i
j
k
l
m
n
o
p
q
r
s
t
u
v
w
x
y
z

front

The **front** of something is the part that you usually see first.

*The driver sits at the **front** of the bus.*

frost   frosts

There is a **frost** when it gets very cold. The ground is covered with thin white ice called **frost**.

frown   frowns, frowning, frowned

When you **frown**, you look angry or worried. Lines appear on your forehead.

*Mum **frowned** when I banged the door.*

froze   See **freeze**.

frozen   See **freeze**.

fruit   fruit or fruits

Fruit is the part of a plant that holds the seeds. Apples, oranges and bananas are **fruit** that you eat.

fry   fries, frying, fried

If you **fry** food, you cook it in hot oil or fat.

full   fuller, fullest

If something is **full**, there is no space left inside it.

*The bucket is **full** of sand.*

full stop   full stops

A **full stop** is a punctuation mark. It looks like a dot and is used at the end of a sentence.

fun

When you have **fun**, you have a good time.

*We had a lot of **fun** at the circus.*

funny   funnier, funniest

1 Something **funny** makes you laugh.

*The clowns were really **funny**.*

2 If something is **funny**, it can be strange in some way.

*Will gave me a **funny** look.*

fur

Fur is the thick, soft hair that grows on the bodies of animals. Bears, rabbits and cats have **fur**.

furniture

Chairs, tables and beds are **furniture**.

furry   furrier, furriest

Something **furry** is covered in thick, soft hair.

further

Further is another word for farther. See **far**.

furthest

Furthest is another word for farthest. See **far**.

future

The **future** is the time that has not come yet.

*Yesterday was in the past, and tomorrow is in the **future**.*

Gg

gale gales
A **gale** is a very strong wind.
The fence was blown down in the gale.

game games
A **game** is something you play for fun, like hide-and-seek. Sports like football are **games** – so is a board **game** like Snakes and Ladders.

gap gaps
A **gap** is an empty space between two things.
Mick has a gap where his tooth fell out.

garage garages
1 A **garage** is a building where you keep a car.
2 You also buy petrol and have your car mended at a **garage**.

garden gardens
A **garden** is a piece of land next to a house. People grow flowers and vegetables in their **gardens**.

gas gases
1 Gas is something that is not solid or liquid. Air is a **gas**.
2 You burn **gas** to heat your home and cook your food.

gate gates
A **gate** is a kind of door in a fence or wall.

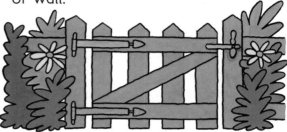

gather gathers, gathering, gathered
When you **gather** things, you bring them together in one place.
The teacher gathered up the books.

gave See **give**.

geese See **goose**.

gentle gentler, gentlest
If you are **gentle**, you are kind and careful.
The nurse was very gentle with the baby.

gentleman gentlemen
Gentleman is a polite word for a man.

gerbil gerbils
A **gerbil** is a small animal that looks like a mouse. **Gerbils** are often kept as pets.

a
b
c
d
e
f

Gg

h
i
j
k
l
m
n
o
p
q
r
s
t
u
v
w
x
y
z

get gets, getting, got
If you **get** something, you fetch it from somewhere.
*It's cold, so I'll **get** my jumper.*

ghost ghosts
A **ghost** looks like a person who is already dead. Some people say they have seen a **ghost**.

giant giants
1 In fairy stories, a **giant** is a very large, strong person.
2 Something very big is called **giant**.
*This is a **giant** packet of cornflakes.*

gigantic
Something **gigantic** is very, very large.
*The boys ate a **gigantic** meal.*

giggle giggles, giggling, giggled
If you **giggle**, you keep on laughing.
*We couldn't stop **giggling** – it was such a good joke!*

giraffe giraffes
A **giraffe** is a tall animal with a very long neck.

girl girls
A **girl** is a child who will grow up to be a woman.
*Your mum used to be a **girl**.*

give gives, giving, gave, given
If you **give** something to someone, you let them have it.
*Sam **gave** Raul an apple.*

glad
When you are **glad**, you are pleased and happy.
*I'm really **glad** Gran's coming to stay.*

glass glasses
1 **Glass** is a hard, clear material that you can see through. Windows and bottles are made of **glass**.
2 A **glass** is a kind of cup made of **glass**.

glasses glasses
You wear **glasses** to help you see better. You look through two special pieces of glass or plastic held in a frame.

gloomy gloomier, gloomiest
1 If you are **gloomy**, you feel sad.
2 **Gloomy** weather is cloudy and rather dark.

glove gloves
You wear **gloves** on your hands to keep them warm. **Gloves** have a separate part for each finger.

glue
You use **glue** to stick things together.
Ben stuck the picture in his book with glue.

go **goes, going, went, gone**
If you **go** somewhere, you move from one place to another.
My brother and I are going to the swimming pool.

goal **goals**
1 You must put the ball in the **goal** to score a point in a game like football.
The crowd roared when the ball shot into the goal.
2 You score a **goal** by putting the ball into the **goal**.
Mark scored a goal with a brilliant header.

goat **goats**
A **goat** is a farm animal. **Goats** are kept for their milk.

gold
Gold is a shiny yellow metal. It is used to make jewellery.

golden
Something **golden** is the colour of gold.
Goldilocks had golden hair.

goldfish **goldfish**
A **goldfish** is a small golden or orange fish. People keep **goldfish** as pets.

gone See **go**.

good **better, best**
1 If you think something is **good**, you like it.
That was a good game!
2 If you are **good** at something, you can do it well.
Jack is very good at reading.
3 A **good** person is kind to others and cares about them.

goodbye
You say **goodbye** to someone when you leave them.

good night
You say **good night** to someone when they go to bed.

goose **geese**
A **goose** is a large bird that swims and flies.

gorilla **gorillas**
A **gorilla** is the largest ape. It has thick black fur and is very strong.

got See **get**.

a
b
c
d
e
f
Gg
h
i
j
k
l
m
n
o
p
q
r
s
t
u
v
w
x
y
z

a
b
c
d
e
f

Gg

h
i
j
k
l
m
n
o
p
q
r
s
t
u
v
w
x
y
z

grab **grabs, grabbing, grabbed**
If you **grab** something, you take hold of it quickly.
Grab your things! We're going swimming.

gram **grams**
You can measure mass in **grams**. There are 1000 **grams** (g) in a kilogram (kg).

grammar
Grammar is the rules of a language. It tells you how words and sentences should be put together.

grandad **grandads**
Grandad is another word for grandfather.

grandfather **grandfathers**
Your **grandfather** is the father of your father or mother.

grandmother **grandmothers**
Your **grandmother**, or **gran**, is the mother of your father or mother.

granny **grannies**
Granny is another word for grandmother.

grape **grapes**
A **grape** is a juicy fruit that grows in a bunch.

grapefruit **grapefruits**
A **grapefruit** is a juicy yellow fruit like a big orange. People eat **grapefruit** for breakfast.

graph **graphs**
A **graph** is a special kind of drawing or diagram that shows information.

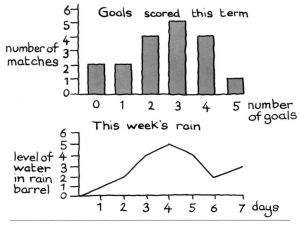

grass
Grass is a plant with thin green leaves. It grows in fields and gardens. Cows and other animals eat **grass**.

great **greater, greatest**
1 Great means very good.
*We had a **great** time at the fair!*
2 Great also means very large.
*There's a **great** black cloud up above us.*
3 Great can also mean important or famous.
*Victoria was a **great** queen.*

greedy **greedier, greediest**
A **greedy** person takes more than they need.

grew See **grow**.

groan groans, groaning, groaned

If you **groan**, you make a long, low sound. You **groan** when something hurts or upsets you.

Mum groaned when she saw the mess.

ground

1 The **ground** is what you walk on.
The plate hit the ground with a crash.
2 **Ground** also means earth or land.
The ground was too hard to dig.

group groups, grouping, grouped

1 A **group** of people or things is a number of them that are all together.
2 If you **group** people or things, you put them together.

grow grows, growing, grew, grown

When something **grows**, it gets bigger.

growl growls, growling, growled

A **growl** is a deep, rough, angry sound made in the throat.
The lion growled angrily.

grown See **grow**.

grown-up grown-ups

A **grown-up** is a person who is not a child. **Grown-ups** are called adults.

guard guards, guarding, guarded

1 If you **guard** something, you watch over it to keep it safe.
2 A **guard** is a person who **guards** someone or something.

guess guesses

If you give an answer when you are not sure it is right, you are making a **guess**.

guide guides, guiding, guided

1 If you **guide** someone, you show them the way to go.
2 A **guide** shows you around somewhere, or leads the way.
We followed the guide through the jungle.

guinea pig guinea pigs

A **guinea pig** is a small, furry animal without a tail. It is often kept as a pet.

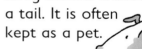

guitar guitars

A **guitar** is a musical instrument with strings. You play it with your fingers.

gun guns

A **gun** is a machine that fires bullets.

a b c d e f **Gg** h i j k l m n o p q r s t u v w x y z

Hh

a b c d e f g **Hh** i j k l m n o p q r s t u v w x y z

had   See **have**.

hail
Hail is drops of hard, icy rain.
The hail bounced off the road.

hair   **hairs**
Your **hair** is what grows on your head. It is made up of lots of **hairs**.
Stacey has curly red hair.

hairy   **hairier, hairiest**
Something covered in hair is **hairy**.

half   **halves**
1 If you divide something equally into two, each part is a **half**.
2 When you say the time, **half** past means 30 minutes past.
Mum's coming home at half past two.

halfway
If you are **halfway** between two places, you are the same distance from each of them.

hall   **halls**
1 The **hall** of a house is just inside the front door.
2 A **hall** can also be a large room or building.
Assembly is held in the school hall.

Halloween
Halloween is the 31st of October. Children like to dress up in costumes.

halve   **halves, halving, halved**
If you divide something exactly in two, you **halve** it.

halves   See **half**.

hammer   **hammers**
A **hammer** is a tool used for hitting nails into wood.

hamster   **hamsters**
A **hamster** is a small, furry animal that looks like a mouse without a tail. It is often kept as a pet.

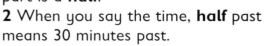

hand   **hands, handing, handed**
1 Your **hand** is at the end of your arm. (See page 174.)
2 If you **hand** something to someone, you give it to them.

handle   **handles**
The **handle** of anything is the part that you hold in your hand.
Alice turned the handle and opened the front door.

handlebars

Handlebars are part of a bicycle. (See page 175.)

handwriting

Your **handwriting** is the writing you do with a pen or pencil.

hang **hangs, hanging, hung**

If you **hang** something, you fix it at the top.

*Please **hang** your coat up.*

Hanukkah **or** Chanukah

Hanukkah is an eight-day Jewish festival of lights.

happen **happens, happening, happened**

If something **happens**, it takes place.

happy **happier, happiest**

When you are **happy**, you are very pleased.

*I was so **happy** on my birthday!*

harbour **harbours**

Boats are tied up in a **harbour** to keep them safe from big waves.

hard **harder, hardest**

1 Something that is **hard** is firm or difficult to break.

*This ice cream is as **hard** as a rock!*

2 Something that is **hard** to do is difficult.

*I can't do this puzzle – it's really **hard**!*

hare **hares**

A **hare** is an animal that looks like a large rabbit. It has long ears and long back legs.

harvest **harvests**

The **harvest** is the gathering of crops when they are ripe.

*At **harvest** time, the corn is cut and taken to the barn.*

has See **have**.

hat **hats**

A **hat** is something you wear on your head.

hatch **hatches, hatching, hatched**

When a baby bird **hatches**, it comes out of its egg.

hate **hates, hating, hated**

If you **hate** something, you do not like it at all.

have **has, having, had**

1 If you **have** something, you own it or it is with you.

*Fred **has** a new bike.*

2 If you **have** done something, you did it in the past.

*I **have** been on an aeroplane before.*

haven't

Haven't is short for have not.

*I **haven't** done it yet – I'll do it tomorrow.*

hay

Hay is dry grass that is used to feed animals.

head **heads**

1 Your **head** is the top part of your body. (See page 174.)

2 The **head** of something is the person in charge.

*The **head** teacher called everyone into the hall.*

headache **headaches**

A **headache** is a pain in the head that goes on hurting.

headlight **headlights**

Headlights are the lights at the front of a car. (See page 175.)

head teacher **head teachers**

The **head teacher** is the teacher in charge of a school.

heal **heals, healing, healed**

When something **heals**, it becomes healthy again.

healthy **healthier, healthiest**

If you are **healthy**, your body is fit and you are not ill.

hear **hears, hearing, heard**

When you **hear** something, you notice the sound it makes.

*I can **hear** music.*

heart **hearts**

Your **heart** is inside your chest. It sends blood round your body.

heat **heats, heating, heated**

1 If you **heat** something, you make it warmer.

*I'll **heat** some soup for lunch.*

2 **Heat** is the warm feeling you get from something hot.

heaven

Heaven is a place of happiness. Some people think you go to **heaven** when you die.

heavy **heavier, heaviest**

A person or thing that is **heavy** weighs a lot.

hedge **hedges**

A **hedge** is a kind of fence between fields or gardens. It is made of small trees and bushes.

hedgehog **hedgehogs**

A **hedgehog** is a small brown animal with sharp spines on its back. It rolls into a ball when it is frightened.

heel **heels**
1 Your **heel** is the back part of your foot. (See page 174.)
2 A **heel** is also part of a shoe.

---

height **heights**
You measure how high something is to find out its **height**.

---

held See **hold**.

---

helicopter **helicopters**
A **helicopter** is a vehicle that flies. It has large blades on top which spin round. **Helicopters** can go straight up into the air.

---

helmet **helmets**
A **helmet** is a hard hat that keeps your head from getting hurt.
*You should always wear a **helmet** when you ride your bike.*

---

help **helps, helping, helped**
When you **help** someone, you do something useful for them.
*I **helped** Dad carry the bags.*

---

hen **hens**
A **hen** is a female chicken. **Hens** lay eggs that people can eat.

---

her
Her means belonging to a girl or woman.
*Mum's coming. I can see **her** car.*

herd **herds, herding, herded**
1 A **herd** is a group of animals of one kind that live together.
*There is a large **herd** of cows on this farm.*

2 If you **herd** animals or people, you move them together as a group.
*The dogs **herded** the sheep into a corner.*

---

here
Here means the place where you are now.
*Have you seen my skateboard? I thought I left it **here**.*

---

hero **heroes**
1 A **hero** is a man or boy who has done something brave or good.
2 The **hero** of a story is the man or boy that it is about.

---

heroine **heroines**
1 A **heroine** is a woman or girl who has done something brave or good.
2 The **heroine** of a story is the woman or girl that it is about.

---

hexagon **hexagons**
A **hexagon** is a flat shape that has six sides.

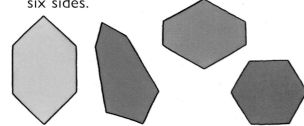

a
b
c
d
e
f
g
Hh
i
j
k
l
m
n
o
p
q
r
s
t
u
v
w
x
y
z

a
b
c
d
e
f
g
Hh
i
j
k
l
m
n
o
p
q
r
s
t
u
v
w
x
y
z

hide **hides, hiding, hid, hidden**
1 If you **hide** something, you put it where no one can find it.
2 If you **hide**, you go where no one can see you.

high **higher, highest**
If something is **high**, it is tall or a long way from the ground.

hill **hills**
A **hill** is land that is higher than the land around it. A **hill** is not as tall as a mountain.

hip **hips**
Your **hip** is where your leg joins your body. (See page 174.)

hippopotamus
hippopotamuses or hippopotami
A **hippopotamus**, or **hippo** for short, is a very large African animal. It lives in or near a river.

his
His means belonging to a boy or a man.
Dan can't find his books.

history
Things that happened in the past are **history**.
We learned about the Romans in our history lesson.

hit **hits, hitting, hit**
If you **hit** something, you touch it very hard.
The ball hit me so hard that I fell over.

hive **hives**
When people keep bees, the bees live in a **hive**.

hold **holds, holding, held**
1 You **hold** something by taking it in your hand.
My friend asked me if I would like to hold his pet hamster.
2 A container **holds** the amount you can fit inside it.
This jar holds 50 sweets.

hole **holes**
A **hole** is an opening or empty space in something.
There is a hole in my jumper.

holiday **holidays**
If you are on **holiday**, you do not have to go to school or work. You may go away for a **holiday**.
We are going camping for our holiday this year.

hollow
Something **hollow** has space inside it.
Owls sometimes build their nests in hollow trees.

holly

Holly is a small tree or bush. It has prickly green leaves and red berries.

home homes

Your **home** is the place where you live.

*My **home** is near the school.*

honest

If you are **honest**, you tell the truth and people trust you.

honey

Honey is a sweet, sticky food made by bees.

hoof hoofs or hooves

A **hoof** is the hard, bony part of a horse's foot. Cows, sheep and goats have **hooves**, too.

hop hops, hopping, hopped

1 When you **hop**, you jump on one foot. When birds **hop**, they jump with both feet together.
2 A **hop** is a small jump.

hope hopes, hoping, hoped

When you **hope** that something will happen, you want it to happen.

*I **hope** I pass the test!*

horn horns

A **horn** is the hard point that sticks out from the heads of some animals.

horrible

If you think something is **horrible**, you do not like it at all.

*Today's pudding was **horrible**!*

horse horses

A **horse** is a large animal that people ride. Some **horses** pull things, and some take part in races.

hospital hospitals

A **hospital** is a large building where ill people are looked after.

hot hotter, hottest

Something **hot** is very warm. Very **hot** things can burn you.

*Be careful! The water is very **hot**.*

a b c d e f g **Hh** i j k l m n o p q r s t u v w x y z

hotel hotels
You can stay in a **hotel** when you are away from home. A **hotel** has lots of bedrooms.

hour hours
An **hour** is made up of 60 minutes. There are 24 **hours** in a day.

house houses
A **house** is a building that people live in. It has several rooms.

how
When you say **how** something happens, you explain the way that it happens.

huge
If something is **huge**, it is very, very big.
An elephant is a huge animal.

human humans
A **human** is a person.

hump humps
A **hump** is a big bump. Camels have **humps**.

hundred hundreds
A **hundred** is the number 100. The number 342 has 3 **hundreds**, 4 tens and 2 units.

hung See **hang**.

hungry hungrier, hungriest
When you are **hungry**, you want something to eat.
I'm hungry! I haven't eaten for hours.

hunt hunts, hunting, hunted
1 When an animal **hunts**, it chases and kills another animal.
Owls hunt for mice at night.
2 When you **hunt** for something, you look everywhere for it.
I'm hunting for my socks.

hurry hurries, hurrying, hurried
If you **hurry**, you move or do something quickly.
We were late, so we hurried to school.

hurt hurts, hurting, hurt
If something **hurts**, you feel pain there.
My arm hurts where I banged it.

husband husbands
A **husband** is a married man.

hut huts
A **hut** is a small building. It is usually made of wood.

hutch hutches
A **hutch** is a kind of cage made from wood and metal. Pet rabbits live in **hutches**.

Ii

ice
Ice is water that has frozen hard.
*Would you like some **ice** in your drink?*

ice cream   ice creams
Ice cream is a sweet, frozen food. It tastes creamy and comes in lots of flavours.

icicle   icicles
An **icicle** is a pointed, hanging piece of ice. It is made when dripping water freezes.
Icicles were hanging from the roof.

idea   ideas
An **idea** is something you have thought of yourself.
*I had a brilliant **idea**!*

igloo   igloos
An **igloo** is a kind of house. It is made from blocks of hard snow or ice.

ill
When you are **ill**, you do not feel very well.
*Kyle was **ill**, so he spent the day in bed.*

illness   illnesses
If you have an **illness**, you do not feel well. Colds and flu are **illnesses**.

illustration   illustrations
An **illustration** is a picture in a book.

illustrator   illustrators
An **illustrator** is someone who draws the pictures in a book.

imagine   imagines, imagining, imagined
If you **imagine** something, you picture it in your mind.

immediately
If something happens **immediately**, it happens straight away.
*Stop that noise **immediately**!*

important
1 If something is **important**, it matters a lot.
*Good health is **important**.*
2 An **important** person has a lot of power.
*A president is an **important** person.*

a b c d e f g h **Ii** j k l m n o p q r s t u v w x y z

impossible

If something is **impossible**, it cannot be done.
*It is **impossible** to walk on water.*

in

1 If someone or something is **in** a place, they are there.
*The PE mats are **in** the cupboard.*
2 If you are **in**, you are at home.

inch   inches

In the past, **inches** were used to measure length.

index   indexes

An **index** is an alphabetical list at the back of a book. It tells you where to find things in the book.

Index

ant	3,10	hedgehog	15
anteater	4,8	hyena	17
antelope	5	lion	8
bear	7,18	monkey	21
camel	9	otter	19
crocodile	10	owl	5
dolphin	6,13	snake	7,29
elephant	2	tortoise	19
flamingo	6	walrus	12
gazelle	25	zebra	32

information

Information about something or someone is the facts about them.
*Have you any **information** about hot-air balloons?*

initial   initials

An **initial** is the first letter of a word or name.
*Sam Brown's **initials** are S.B.*

ink   inks

Ink is a coloured liquid. It is used for printing or writing.

insect   insects

An **insect** is a tiny animal with six legs. **Insects** usually have wings. Flies and ants are **insects**.

inside   insides

The **inside** of something is surrounded by the rest of it.
*Open the box and look **inside** it!*

instruction   instructions

Instructions are words or drawings that tell you what to do.
*I followed the **instructions** on the packet.*

instrument   instruments

1 An **instrument** is a tool people use to do a job.
*The doctor used an **instrument** to look down my ear.*
2 You play a musical **instrument** to make music. Recorders and violins are musical **instruments**.

interesting

If something is **interesting**, you want to know more about it.
*The film was so **interesting** that we watched it again.*

Internet

You can look things up on the **Internet** using a computer.

interrupt   interrupts, interrupting, interrupted

If you start talking when someone is speaking, you **interrupt** them.
*Don't **interrupt** – let Ellie finish what she is saying!*

invent   invents, inventing, invented

If you **invent** something, you are the first person to think of it.
*Alexander Graham Bell **invented** the telephone.*

investigate   investigates, investigating, investigated

If you **investigate** something, you try to find out all about it.
*We are **investigating** what happens when you mix different colours.*

invisible

If something is **invisible**, you cannot see it.
*The school was **invisible** from the road.*

invitation   invitations

You get an **invitation** when someone asks you to their party.

invite   invites, inviting, invited

If you **invite** someone to a party, you ask them to come to it.

iron   irons

1 Iron is a strong, hard, grey metal.
2 People use a hot **iron** to smooth clothes.

island   islands

(*sounds like* eye-land) An **island** is a piece of land that has water all around it.

its

Its means belonging to it.
*My bike has lost **its** wheel.*

it's

It's is short for it is or it has.
It's an interesting book.
It's stopped raining now.

a
b
c
d
e
f
g
h
i
Jj
k
l
m
n
o
p
q
r
s
t
u
v
w
x
y
z

jacket jackets
A **jacket** is a short coat.

jam jams
1 Jam is a sweet food. It is made from fruit and sugar.
I had strawberry jam on my toast.
2 There is also a **jam** when it is so crowded that nothing can move.
The car was stuck in a traffic jam.

January
January is the first month of the year. It has 31 days.

jar jars
A **jar** is a glass container with a wide top. It is used for storing food, such as jam.

jaw jaws
Your **jaw** is one of the bones that hold your teeth.

jeans
Jeans are trousers made from a strong cotton material. They are often blue. (See page 176.)

jelly jellies
Jelly is a soft, sweet food that you can see through.

jet jets
1 A **jet** is an aeroplane that can fly very fast and very high.
2 A **jet** is also a narrow stream of something.
A jet of water shot out through the hole in the pipe.

jewel jewels
A **jewel** is a beautiful, shiny stone that costs a lot of money. Diamonds and emeralds are **jewels**.

jewellery
Rings, necklaces and earrings are **jewellery**. **Jewellery** is often made of gold or silver, sometimes with jewels.

jigsaw jigsaws
A **jigsaw** is a puzzle. You fit together shapes to make a picture.
This jigsaw has 100 pieces.

job jobs
1 A **job** is something you have to do.
It's my job to collect the books.
2 A **job** is also work that you are paid to do.
My mum has a job as a bus driver.

join joins, joining, joined

1 When you **join** things, you put them together.

2 If you **join** a club, you become a member of it.
*Sophie has **joined** the swimming club.*

joint joints

A **joint** is a part of the body where two bones fit together.
*Your finger **joints** are called knuckles.*

joke jokes

A **joke** is something that you say to make people laugh.

journey journeys

If you go on a **journey**, you travel from one place to another.

jug jugs

A **jug** is a container for holding liquids. It has a handle and a lip for pouring.

juice juices

Juice is the liquid that can be squeezed out of fruit.
*I drink orange **juice** at breakfast.*

July

July is the seventh month of the year. It has 31 days.

jump jumps, jumping, jumped

You **jump** when you move yourself into the air.
*Tim **jumped** off the wall.*

jumper jumpers

A **jumper** is a piece of clothing with sleeves. You wear it on the top half of your body to keep you warm.

June

June is the sixth month of the year. It has 30 days.

jungle jungles

A **jungle** is a thick forest in a hot country.

just

If something has **just** happened, it happened a very short time ago.
*I **just** got to school a minute ago.*

kangaroo kangaroos

A **kangaroo** is a large Australian animal. It jumps on its strong back legs. Female **kangaroos** carry their babies in a pocket on their stomachs.

keep keeps, keeping, kept

1 If you **keep** something, you save it.
I'll keep the last sweet for you.
2 If you **keep** something somewhere, you always put it there.
I keep all my books in the bookcase.

kennel kennels

A **kennel** is a small shed for a dog to sleep in.

kept See **keep**.

ketchup

Ketchup is a cold sauce made from tomatoes.

kettle kettles

People boil water in a **kettle**.

key keys, keying, keyed

1 A **key** is a piece of metal with a special shape. It opens a lock.
2 You press the **keys** on a piano or a computer with your fingers.
3 If you **key** in information on a computer keyboard, you type it in.

keyboard keyboards

A **keyboard** is all the keys on a computer or piano.

kick kicks, kicking, kicked

If you **kick** something, you hit it hard with your foot.
Malik kicked the ball into the air.

kid kids

1 A **kid** is a young goat.
2 Children are often called **kids**.

kill kills, killing, killed

If somebody **kills** something, they make it die.
The fox killed the chicken.

kilogram or kilo kilograms or kilos

You can measure mass in **kilograms** or **kilos**. A **kilogram** (kg) is 1000 grams.

kilometre kilometres

You can measure distance in **kilometres**. A **kilometre** (km) is 1000 metres.

kind kinder, kindest; kinds

1 A **kind** person is caring and helpful.
It was kind of Harry to lend me his bike.
2 Things of the same **kind** are part of the same group.
Cars and bikes are kinds of vehicles.

king kings

A **king** is a man who rules a country because he belongs to a royal family.

kingdom **kingdoms**
A **kingdom** is the area that is ruled by a king or queen.

kiss **kisses, kissing, kissed**
When you **kiss** someone, you touch them with your lips.
Mum kissed me on the cheek.

kitchen **kitchens**
A **kitchen** is a room where food is cooked.

kite **kites**
A **kite** is a toy that you fly in the air. It is tied to a long piece of string.

kitten **kittens**
A **kitten** is a young cat.

knee **knees**
Your **knee** is the part of your leg that bends. (See page 174.)

kneel **kneels, kneeling knelt or kneeled**
When you **kneel**, you get down on your knees.

knew See **know**.

knickers
Knickers are pants worn by women and girls. (See page 176.)

knife **knives**
A **knife** is a tool for cutting things. It has a handle and a sharp blade.

knight **knights**
Hundreds of years ago, a **knight** was a soldier who wore armour and rode a horse.

knit **knits, knitting, knitted**
When you **knit**, you make clothes using wool and a pair of long needles.

knives See **knife**.

knock **knocks, knocking, knocked**
1 If you **knock** something, you hit it hard.
2 If you **knock** on a door, you make a noise to tell people you are there.

knot **knots**
A **knot** is made by tying two pieces of string together.

know **knows, knowing, knew, known**
1 If you **know** something, it is in your mind and you do not need to learn it.
2 If you **know** someone, you have met them before.

koala **koalas**
A **koala** is a small Australian animal.

a b c d e f g h i j **Kk** l m n o p q r s t u v w x y z

81

a
b
c
d
e
f
g
h
i
j
k
Ll
m
n
o
p
q
r
s
t
u
v
w
x
y
z

label labels

A **label** is a small notice that tells you more about something.

lace laces

1 Lace is another word for shoelace.
2 Lace is also a kind of pretty cloth with lots of holes in it.

ladder ladders

You climb up a **ladder** to reach something high. **Ladders** are made of metal or wood.

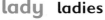

lady ladies

Lady is a polite word for a woman.

ladybird ladybirds

A **ladybird** is a small red beetle with black spots. It is often found in gardens.

laid See **lay**.

lain See **lie**[2].

lake lakes

A **lake** is a large area of fresh water with land all around it.

lamb lambs

A **lamb** is a young sheep.

lamp lamps

You turn on a **lamp** to give you light when it is dark.

land lands, landing, landed

1 When you **land** somewhere, you arrive after a journey by aeroplane.
*We **landed** at the airport.*
2 Land is the dry part of the Earth not covered by water.

lane lanes

A **lane** is a narrow road.

language languages

Language is the words people use to speak and write. People in different countries speak different **languages**.

lap laps, lapping, lapped

1 When you sit down, the tops of your legs make your **lap**.
*The cat likes to sit on my **lap**.*
2 An animal **laps** when it drinks using its tongue.
*The cat **lapped** up its milk.*

large larger, largest
If something is **large**, it is big.
Katie and I shared a large drink.

last lasts, lasting, lasted
1 When something is **last**, it comes at the end.
The last month of the year is December.
2 If something **lasts**, it goes on for some time.
This film lasts an hour.

late later, latest
1 If you are **late**, you arrive after you are expected.
2 The **late** part of something is near the end.
We'll get there by late afternoon.

laugh laughs, laughing, laughed
When you **laugh**, you make a sound to show that something is funny.
We all laughed at the clown.

law laws
A **law** is a rule that everyone in a country must follow.
Dropping litter is against the law.

lawn lawns
A **lawn** is the grass that grows next to a house.

lay lays, laying, laid
1 If you **lay** something down, you put it down carefully.
Please lay your pencils down on the table.
2 If you **lay** the table, you get it ready for a meal.
3 When a hen **lays** an egg, it pushes it out of its body.
See **lie**².

layer layers
A **layer** is something flat that goes above or below something else.
Mum covered the carpet with a layer of newspaper.

lazy lazier, laziest
A **lazy** person does not want to work.
I feel too lazy to get out of bed!

lead leads, leading, led
1 (*sounds like* seed) If you **lead** someone, you go in front of them to show the way.
You lead and we'll follow.
2 (*sounds like* seed) If you **lead** in a race, you are in front of the other runners.
Joe was leading the others until the last few metres.
3 (*sounds like* seed) A **lead** is a long piece of leather that you fix to a dog's collar.
4 (*sounds like* red) **Lead** is a heavy, soft grey metal.
5 (*sounds like* red) The **lead** of a pencil is the part which makes marks.

leader leaders
The **leader** of a group is in charge of it.
The captain is the leader of the team.

a
b
c
d
e
f
g
h
i
j
k
Ll
m
n
o
p
q
r
s
t
u
v
w
x
y
z

a
b
c
d
e
f
g
h
i
j
k
Ll
m
n
o
p
q
r
s
t
u
v
w
x
y
z

leaf leaves
A **leaf** is a flat, green part of a tree or plant. **Leaves** grow out of branches or stems.

lean leans, leaning, leaned, leant
If you **lean**, you bend in one direction.
*That tree **leans** over the road.*

leap leaps, leaping, leapt or leaped
1 If you **leap**, you jump a long way.
*Megan **leapt** across the stream.*
2 In a **leap year**, February has 29 days instead of 28.

learn learns, learning, learned, learnt
When you **learn** something, you get to know something new.
*I am **learning** to ride a bike.*

least
Least means the smallest amount.
Sarah and Ian ate most of the popcorn –
*I had the **least**.*

leather
Leather is made from the skin of animals. Shoes and bags can be made of **leather**.

leave leaves, leaving, left
1 When you **leave** a place, you go away from it.
2 If you **leave** something somewhere, you do not take it with you.

leaves See **leaf** and **leave**.

led See **lead**.

left
Left is the opposite of right. When you read or write, you start at the **left** side of the page.
*Tom has his **left** foot on the ball.*

leg legs
Your **legs** are parts of your body. (See page 174.)

lemon lemons
A **lemon** is a small yellow fruit. It has a very sharp flavour.

lemonade
Lemonade is a cold drink that is made from lemons, sugar and water.

lend lends, lending, lent
When someone **lends** you something, they give it to you for a short time. Then you give it back.
*Please will you **lend** me your pencil sharpener?*

length lengths
You measure how long something is to find out its **length**.

lent See **lend**.

less

Less means not as much.
*If you have a large drink and I have a small drink, I have **less** than you.*

lesson lessons

A **lesson** is a time when you are taught something.
*I had a swimming **lesson** today.*

let lets, letting, let

If someone **lets** you do something, they say you may do it.
*Nicky **let** me ride her bicycle.*

letter letters

1 A **letter** is a written message.
*I wrote a **letter** to my granny in Australia.*
2 A **letter** is one of the symbols you use to write words.
*A B C D are capital **letters** and a b c d are lower-case **letters**.*

lettuce lettuces

Lettuce is a green vegetable. Its leaves are often used in salad.

level

If something is **level**, it is flat.
*A table needs to be **level**.*

library libraries

A **library** is a place where lots of books are kept. You can borrow books from a **library** to read at home.

lick licks, licking, licked

If you **lick** something, you move your tongue across it.
*The dog **licked** the bowl clean.*

lid lids

A **lid** is a cover on a container. You take off the **lid** to open the container.
*Tim took the **lid** off the pan.*

lie¹ lies, lying, lied

If you **lie** or tell a **lie**, you say something which you know is not true.

lie² lies, lying, lay, lain

If you **lie** down, you rest your body flat on something.
*Our cat **lies** in the sun all day.*

life lives

Your **life** is the time when you are alive. The **life** of a person or animal begins when they are born and ends when they die.

lifeboat lifeboats

A **lifeboat** is a boat that goes to save people who are in danger at sea.

lift lifts, lifting, lifted

1 If you **lift** something, you pick it up and move it upwards.
*I'll **lift** that heavy box for you.*
2 A **lift** carries people up and down in a building.

a
b
c
d
e
f
g
h
i
j
k
Ll
m
n
o
p
q
r
s
t
u
v
w
x
y
z

light lights, lighting, lit; lighter, lightest

1 Light comes from the sun during the day.

2 A **light** is a lamp that you turn on to help you see when it is dark.

3 If you **light** something, you make it start to burn.

4 Something **light** is not heavy.

5 A **light** colour is pale.

lighthouse lighthouses

A **lighthouse** is a tower with a bright, flashing light at the top. It warns ships of dangerous rocks.

lightning

Lightning is a very bright flash of light in the sky during a thunderstorm.

like likes, liking, liked

1 If you **like** someone, you think they are very nice.

2 If one thing is **like** another, it is the same in some way.

*Sam's bike is **like** mine.*

likely likelier, likeliest

Something that is **likely** will probably happen.

*Susie works hard, so she's **likely** to do well.*

line lines

1 A **line** is a long, thin mark. **Lines** can be straight or curved.

*Put a **line** under the date.*

2 A **line** is also a row of people or things.

*We wait in a **line** for our dinner.*

lion lions

A **lion** is a large wild cat. It eats other animals.

lip lips

Your **lips** are the parts of your face around your mouth. (See page 174.)

liquid liquids

A **liquid** is something that pours easily and is not solid. Water, milk, oil and fruit juice are all **liquids**.

list lists

If you make a **list**, you write things down one after another.

*Mum wrote the things she needed on a shopping **list**.*

listen listens, listening, listened

When you **listen**, you try to hear something.

lit See **light**.

litre litres

You can measure liquid in **litres**.

A **litre** (l) is 1000 millilitres (ml).

*Can I have a **litre** of milk, please?*

litter

Litter is rubbish that people drop on the ground.
Please take your litter home with you.

little   less, least

1 If something is **little**, it is small.
Grandad gave some milk to the little kitten.
2 A **little** means only a small amount.
Grandad only gave the kitten a little milk.

live   lives, living, lived

1 If you **live,** you are alive and breathing.
2 If you **live** in a place, your home is there.
David lives in Wales.

lives   See **life** and **live**.

lizard   lizards

A **lizard** is a reptile with four legs and a long tail. **Lizards** have rough, dry skins.

load   loads, loading, loaded

When you **load** a vehicle, you put lots of things on it or in it.
We loaded the car with suitcases.

loaf   loaves

You can cut a **loaf** of bread into slices. Some **loaves** are already sliced.

local

If something is **local**, it is near to your home.
I go to the local school.

lock   locks, locking, locked

1 If something is **locked**, you need a key to open it.
2 A **lock** keeps a door or suitcase shut. It can only be opened with the right key.

log   logs

A **log** is a large piece of wood from a tree.

lollipop   lollipops

A **lollipop** is a hard sweet on a stick. It is also called a lolly.

lolly   lollies

1 **Lolly** is another word for lollipop.
2 A **lolly** is also a piece of flavoured ice or ice cream on a stick.

lonely   lonelier, loneliest

If you are **lonely**, you are unhappy because you are alone.
My gran gets lonely, so I often go to see her.

long   longer, longest

1 Something **long** is a great distance from end to end.
2 A **long** time is a great amount of time. **Long** ago means many years ago.

a
b
c
d
e
f
g
h
i
j
k
Ll
m
n
o
p
q
r
s
t
u
v
w
x
y
z

look looks, looking, looked
1 If you **look** at something, you turn your eyes towards it so you can see it.
I looked at my dirty hands.
2 If you **look** for something, you try to find it.
Peter looked everywhere for his coat.

loose looser, loosest
Something that is **loose** moves about.
Sasha has a loose tooth.

lorry lorries
A **lorry** is a large vehicle. It carries big things by road.

lose loses, losing, lost
1 If you **lose** something, you cannot find it.
I've lost my book. I don't know where it is!
2 If you **lose** a race, you do not come first.

lost
If you are **lost**, you do not know where you are.
We were lost, so we asked the way.
See **lose**.

lot lots
A **lot** means a large number or amount.
There are a lot of boys in my class.

loud louder, loudest
Something **loud** is very noisy.
The music got louder as the band came up the road.

love loves, loving, loved
1 Love is a very strong feeling of liking for someone.
2 If you **love** someone, you like them very, very much.

lovely lovelier, loveliest
Something **lovely** is very nice to see, hear, smell or do.
That music is lovely!
I had a lovely birthday.

low lower, lowest
Something **low** is not very high.

lucky luckier, luckiest
If you are **lucky**, good things seem to happen to you.
I'm really lucky – I've got a new bike!

lump lumps
A **lump** is a solid piece of something.
Mum put a few lumps of coal on the fire.

lunch lunches
Lunch is the meal that you eat in the middle of the day.

lying See **lie.**

Mm

machine machines

A **machine** makes things or does a job. **Machines** often use electricity.
Our dirty clothes go into the washing machine.

made See **make**.

magazine magazines

A **magazine** is a thin book with lots of pictures. It usually comes out once a week or once a month.

magic

In fairy stories, **magic** things happen that could not happen in real life.
Cinderella's rags turned into a beautiful dress by magic!

magician magicians

A **magician** does clever tricks that seem impossible.
The magician pulled a rabbit out of an empty hat.

magnet magnets

A **magnet** is a special piece of metal that some metal things stick to.

main

The **main** thing is the most important one.
The bank is on the main street.

make makes, making, made

1 When you **make** something, you put things together until you have something new.
We made a den out of boxes.
2 If you are **made** to do something, somebody sees that you do it.
My mum made me put my coat on.

male males

A **male** person or animal can be a father. Boys and men are **males**.

mammal mammals

A **mammal** is an animal that feeds its babies with its own milk. People, whales and cats are all **mammals**.

man men

A **man** is a grown-up male person.

manage manages, managing, managed

When you **manage** to do something, you are able to do something difficult.

many

Many means a lot of.
*There are **many** words in this dictionary.*

map maps

A **map** is a drawing that helps you find your way around.

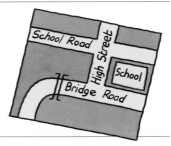

March

March is the third month of the year. It has 31 days.

mark marks, marking, marked

1 A **mark** is a spot or scratch that spoils something.
2 Your teacher gives you a **mark** for your work.
3 Your teacher **marks** your work to say whether it is right or wrong.

market markets

A **market** is a place where people buy and sell things.

marmalade

Marmalade is a kind of jam, usually made from oranges.

married

A **married** person has a husband or a wife.

marry marries, marrying, married

When two people **marry**, they become each other's husband and wife.

mask masks

You wear a **mask** over your face to make you look different.

mass

The **mass** of something is how much there is or how heavy it is.

mat mats

A **mat** is a thick piece of material. It protects a surface or makes it softer.

match matches, matching, matched

1 A **match** is a game between two teams.
2 A **match** is a little stick that people use to light a fire.
3 If you put similar things together, you **match** them.

material materials

1 **Material** is the stuff that things are made of. Metal, glass, wood and plastic are **materials**.
2 **Material** is also the cloth that is used to make things like clothes.

matter matters, mattered

If something **matters**, it is important.

mattress mattresses

A **mattress** is the thick, soft part of a bed that you sleep on.

may

1 If something **may** happen, it is possible that it will happen.
2 If someone says you **may** do something, you are allowed to do it.

May

May is the fifth month of the year. It has 31 days.

meal meals

You have a **meal** when you sit down and eat. Breakfast and dinner are both **meals**.

mean means, meaning, meant; meaner, meanest

1 If you know what something **means**, you are able to explain it.
*A dictionary explains what words **mean**.*
2 If you **mean** to do something, you plan to do it.
*I didn't **mean** to push you.*
3 A **mean** person is unkind and selfish.
*Don't be **mean** – share it with Ed!*

meanwhile

Meanwhile means while something else is happening.

measles

If you have **measles**, you have a fever and lots of red spots.

measure measures, measuring, measured

1 If you **measure** something, you find out its size. (See page 183.)

2 A **measure** is something you use when you **measure**, like a ruler or a jug.

meat

Meat is food that comes from part of an animal.

medicine medicines

When you are ill, you take **medicine** to make you better.

medium

Medium means neither large nor small.

meet meets, meeting, met

If you **meet** someone, you are in the same place at the same time.
*We will **meet** Sue at the station at midday.*

melon melons

A **melon** is a large, round, juicy fruit. It has yellow or green skin.

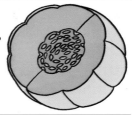

melt melts, melting, melted

When a solid **melts**, it changes into a liquid because it has been heated.
*The sun **melted** my lolly.*

a
b
c
d
e
f
g
h
i
j
k
l

Mm

n
o
p
q
r
s
t
u
v
w
x
y
z

memory **memories**
You use your **memory** when you remember things.
*You learned that quickly – you have a good **memory**!*

men See **man**.

mend **mends, mending, mended**
If you **mend** something that is broken, you put it right.
*When I broke my radio, Mum **mended** it.*

mental
Something **mental** is done in your head.
*When you do **mental** maths, you work out the answer in your head.*

menu **menus**
1 A **menu** in a restaurant is a list of what you can order to eat.
2 A **menu** on a computer screen is a list of things you can choose from.

mess
Things in a **mess** are untidy.

message **messages**
You send or leave a **message** when you cannot speak to someone yourself.
*Dad left a **message** to say he'll be early.*

messy **messier, messiest**
If something is **messy**, it is dirty or untidy.

met See **meet**.

metal **metals**
Metal is a hard, cold material. Steel is a **metal** used to make cars. Gold is a **metal** used to make jewellery.

method **methods**
A **method** is a way of doing something.

metre **metres**
You can measure length in **metres**. There are 100 centimetres (cm) in a **metre** (m).
*John is 1 **metre** 50 centimetres tall.*

mice See **mouse**.

microwave **microwaves**
A **microwave** oven cooks food very quickly.

midday
Midday means 12 o'clock in the middle of the day.

middle **middles**
The **middle** of something is between its edges or ends.
*The cat is in the **middle** of the rug.*

midnight
Midnight means 12 o'clock at night.

might

If something **might** happen, it is possible that it will.

mile **miles**

A **mile** is a way to measure distance. A **mile** is longer than a kilometre.

milk

Milk is a white liquid. Female mammals make **milk** in their bodies to feed their babies. The **milk** that you drink comes from cows.

millennium **millennia**

A **millennium** is 1000 years.

millilitre **millilitres**

You can measure liquid in **millilitres**. There are 1000 **millilitres** (ml) in a litre (l).

millimetre **millimetres**

You can measure length in **millimetres**. There are 10 **millimetres** (mm) in a centimetre (cm), and 1000 **millimetres** in a metre (m).

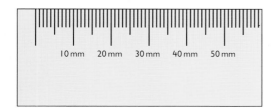

mind **minds, minding, minded**

1 Your **mind** is your thoughts and memories.
2 If you **mind** about something, you care about it.
3 If you **mind** something for someone, you look after it.
*Could you **mind** my bag for a minute?*

mine

Mine means belonging to me.
*That pen is yours and this pen is **mine**.*

minus

Minus is another word you can use when you take away or subtract. The symbol − means **minus**.

minute **minutes**

A **minute** is made up of 60 seconds. There are 60 **minutes** in an hour.

mirror **mirrors**

A **mirror** is a special piece of glass. When you look in a **mirror**, you see yourself.

miss **misses, missing, missed**

1 If you **miss** a bus or train, you arrive too late to catch it.
2 If you try to hit something and **miss**, you do not hit it.
3 If you **miss** someone, you feel sad because they are not with you.

Miss

Miss can be used before the name of a girl or unmarried woman.

missing

If something is **missing**, it is lost.

mistake **mistakes**

A **mistake** is something that is wrong.
*Well done! You have made no **mistakes**.*

a
b
c
d
e
f
g
h
i
j
k
l

Mm

n
o
p
q
r
s
t
u
v
w
x
y
z

a
b
c
d
e
f
g
h
i
j
k
l

Mm

n
o
p
q
r
s
t
u
v
w
x
y
z

mix mixes, mixing, mixed
When you **mix** things, you put them together to make something new.
Mix blue and yellow paint to make green.

mixture mixtures
A **mixture** is a number of different things put together.
*This green paint is a **mixture** of blue and yellow.*

mobile phone mobile phones
A **mobile phone** is a telephone that people can carry.

model models
A **model** is a small copy of something. It shows what it looks like or how it works.
*Dan's building a **model** aeroplane.*

modern
If something is **modern**, it is new and uses the latest ideas and equipment.

mole moles
1 A **mole** is a small, furry animal with tiny eyes. It lives under the ground.
2 A **mole** is also a small, dark spot on someone's skin.

moment moments
A **moment** is a very short time.
*Jenny stopped for a **moment** to pull up her socks.*

Monday Mondays
Monday is the day of the week between Sunday and Tuesday.

money
Money is the notes and coins you use to pay for things.

monkey monkeys
A **monkey** is a small animal with a long tail. **Monkeys** live in hot countries and can climb trees.

monster monsters
In stories, a **monster** is a huge, frightening creature.

month months
A **month** has 28 to 31 days. There are 12 **months** in a year.

moon moons
You see the **moon** shining in the sky at night. The **moon** moves around the Earth once every four weeks.

mop mops
A **mop** is a long handle with strips of cloth joined to the end. You use a **mop** to wash the floor.

more
If someone has **more** than you, they have a larger number or amount than you have.

morning mornings
Morning is the first part of the day. You get up in the **morning**.

mosque mosques
A **mosque** is a building where people go to pray.

most
The person who has **most** has more than anyone else.
Richard has more books than me, but Hirani has the ***most***.

moth moths
A **moth** is an insect that looks like a butterfly. It usually flies around at night.

mother mothers
A **mother** is a woman who has had a child.

motorbike motorbikes
A **motorbike** is a vehicle with two wheels and an engine.

motorway motorways
A **motorway** is a wide road. People going a long way often use a **motorway**.

mountain mountains
A **mountain** is a very high hill. It is very steep and difficult to climb.
Mount Everest is the highest ***mountain*** *in the world.*

mouse mice
1 A **mouse** is a small animal with a long tail and sharp teeth.
2 You use a **mouse** to control the pointer on a computer screen.

mouth mouths
You eat and speak with your **mouth**. It is part of your face. (See page 174.)

move moves, moving, moved
If you **move**, you go to a different place or position.

movement movements
When a person or thing moves, it makes a **movement**.

Mr
Mr can be used before a man's name.

Mrs
Mrs can be used before the name of a married woman.

Ms
Ms can be used before the name of an unmarried or married woman.

much
Much means a lot.

mud
Mud is a wet and sticky mixture of earth and water.

a b c d e f g h i j k l **Mm** n o p q r s t u v w x y z

a
b
c
d
e
f
g
h
i
j
k
l

Mm

n
o
p
q
r
s
t
u
v
w
x
y
z

muddy muddier, muddiest

If something is **muddy**, it is covered with wet earth.

Take off those muddy shoes!

mug mugs

A **mug** is a large cup that you use without a saucer.

multiple multiples

When you multiply a number, you get a **multiple** of it.

6, 9 and 12 are all multiples of 3.

multiplication

Multiplication is a quick way to add together lots of groups of the same number. The symbol × is for **multiplication**.

multiply multiplies, multiplying, multiplied

You **multiply** when you do multiplication.

2 multiplied by 3 is 6.

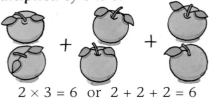

$2 \times 3 = 6$ or $2 + 2 + 2 = 6$

mum or mummy mums or mummies

Mum or **mummy** is what you call your mother.

munch munches, munching, munched

If you **munch**, you chew noisily.

muscle muscles

Muscles are the parts inside your body that you use when you move.

You can feel a muscle in your arm when you bend it.

museum museums

You go to a **museum** to see lots of interesting things.

I saw a rocket at the Science Museum.

mushroom mushrooms

A **mushroom** is a plant with no leaves. You sometimes find **mushrooms** growing among grass.

music

Music is sounds made by people singing or playing instruments like pianos and recorders.

must

If someone **must** do something, they have to do it.

You must look before you cross the road!

my

My means belonging to me.

This is my bat and that is yours.

mystery mysteries

A **mystery** is something that people cannot explain or understand.

How my hamster escaped is a mystery!

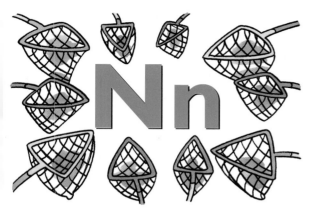

nail   nails
1 Your **nails** are the hard parts at the ends of your fingers and toes.
2 A **nail** is a piece of metal with a pointed end. It is used to join two pieces of wood together.

name   names
A **name** is what you call a person, place or thing.
*My **name** is Josie.*
*The **name** of France's capital city is Paris.*

narrow   narrower, narrowest
Something that is **narrow** measures very little between one side and the other.

nasty   nastier, nastiest
Something **nasty** is not nice.

natural
Something that is **natural** is not made by people or machines.
*Wood and cotton are **natural** materials, but plastic is not.*

nature
Nature is everything in the world that is not made by people. Wild animals, mountains and the weather are part of **nature**.

naughty   naughtier, naughtiest
A **naughty** child behaves badly.

near   nearer, nearest
Something **near** is not far away.

nearly
Nearly means not quite.
*Tara's **nearly** old enough to go to school.*
*Harry **nearly** fell over.*

neat   neater, neatest
If something is **neat**, it is tidy.
*Callum has folded his clothes into a **neat** pile.*

neck   necks
Your **neck** joins your head to the rest of your body. (See page 174.)

necklace   necklaces
A **necklace** is a piece of jewellery that is worn around the neck.

need   needs, needing, needed
If you **need** something, you must have it.
*I **need** a bag to carry my books.*

needle   needles
A **needle** is a thin piece of metal with a point. **Needles** are used for sewing. Special **needles** are used for knitting.

a b c d e f g h i j k l m **Nn** o p q r s t u v w x y z

neighbour neighbours

A **neighbour** is someone who lives very near you.

nephew nephews

A person's **nephew** is the son of their brother or sister.

nervous

If you are **nervous**, you feel worried or afraid.

nest nests

A **nest** is the home that some animals make for their young ones.

net nets

1 **Net** is a material with lots of holes. It is made of knotted thread or string.
2 A **net** is used to catch fish, or in some games like tennis and football.
The ball shot into the back of the net.

nettle nettles

A **nettle** is a wild plant. It has rough leaves that sting.

never

If something **never** happens, it does not happen at any time.
Greg never gets to school on time.

new newer, newest

1 Something **new** has not been used before.
2 **New** also means different.
We did something new today – we played rounders.

news

News is information about things that have just happened.
I've got some exciting news! I won my race!

newspaper newspapers

A **newspaper** tells you in words and pictures what has happened in the world.

next

1 **Next** means the one nearest to you.
I spoke to the girl at the next table.
2 **Next** also means the one that comes after this one.
I'll see you next week.

nice nicer, nicest

If something or someone is **nice**, you like them.

niece nieces

A person's **niece** is the daughter of their brother or sister.

night nights

Night is the time when it is dark and most people sleep.
Did you see the stars last night?

nightdress   nightdresses
A **nightdress** is a loose dress that girls and women wear in bed. (See page 176.)

nightmare   nightmares
A **nightmare** is a frightening dream.

no
1 If you say **no**, you do not agree with someone or you will not do something.
2 No also means none at all.
*My uncle has **no** children.*

nobody
Nobody means no person or no one.
*I opened the door but **nobody** was there.*

nod   nods, nodding, nodded
When you **nod**, you move your head up and down quickly.

noise   noises
Noise is the sounds that someone or something makes.
*The **noise** of the storm kept me awake.*

noisy   noisier, noisiest
Something **noisy** makes a lot of noise.

none
None means not one.
*Sunil has 12 pencils but I have **none**.*

non-fiction
Non-fiction books tell you about real people and things.

nonsense
If someone talks **nonsense**, what they say does not mean anything.

noon
Noon means 12 o'clock in the middle of the day.

no one or no-one
No one means not one person or nobody.
*I opened the door but **no one** was there.*

north
North is a direction. It is on your left when you look towards the rising sun in the morning.

nose   noses
Your **nose** is part of your face. You breathe and smell through your **nose**. (See page 174.)

nostril   nostrils
Your **nostrils** are the two holes in your nose that you breathe through.

a
b
c
d
e
f
g
h
i
j
k
l
m
Nn
o
p
q
r
s
t
u
v
w
x
y
z

note notes

1 A **note** is a short letter.
2 You make **notes** to help you remember something.
3 A **note** is also a piece of paper money.
4 A **note** can also be a single sound in music.

nothing

If you do not have anything, you have **nothing**.

notice notices, noticing, noticed

1 If you **notice** something, you see it and start to think about it.
2 A **notice** is a sign that tells people something.
*The **notice** said: "Keep off the grass".*

noun nouns

A **noun** is a word for a person, animal, place or thing.

November

November is the eleventh month of the year. It has 30 days.

now

Now means at the present time.
*You are reading these words **now**.*

nowhere

Nowhere means not any place.
*We have **nowhere** to play football when the park is closed.*

number numbers

A **number** can be written using letters or symbols. You use **numbers** to count things or people.
*You can see more **numbers** on page 183.*

*You can see more **numbers** on page 183.*

3 three
four 4 **ten** 10
seven 7
six 6 **two** 2

nurse nurses

A **nurse** looks after ill people. **Nurses** usually work in hospitals.

nursery nurseries

1 A **nursery** is a place where young children go to play and learn.
2 A **nursery** school is a school for children from three to five years old.

nursery rhyme
nursery rhymes

A **nursery rhyme** is a poem or song for young children.

nut nuts

A **nut** is a dry brown seed inside a hard shell. It grows on a tree.

oak oaks
An **oak** is a large tree. It has seeds called acorns. Its hard wood is often used to make furniture.

oar oars
An **oar** is a long pole with a flat end. You pull on an **oar** to move a boat through water.

oats
Oats are the seeds of a plant. They are used to make food for people and animals.

obey obeys, obeying, obeyed
When you **obey** someone, you do what they say.

ocean oceans
An **ocean** is a huge sea.

o'clock
You use **o'clock** when you say a time that is exactly on the hour.
*Five **o'clock** means exactly five hours after noon or midnight.*

octagon octagons
An **octagon** is a flat shape that has eight sides. (See page 184.)

October
October is the tenth month of the year. It has 31 days.

octopus octopuses
An **octopus** is a sea creature. It catches food with its eight long arms.

odd odder, oddest
1 An **odd** number cannot be divided exactly by two. There will always be one left over.
2 Something **odd** is a bit strange.

off
1 If you take **off** your coat, you do not wear it any more.
2 If a light or machine is **off**, it is not switched on.
3 When you get **off** something, you are not on it any more.
*We get **off** the bus at the next stop.*

offer offers, offering, offered
If you **offer** something to someone, you ask if they would like it.
*I **offered** Ronan some ice cream.*

office offices
An **office** is a room where people work.

often
Often means many times.
*We **often** have a picnic outside in the summer.*

a
b
c
d
e
f
g
h
i
j
k
l
m
n
Oo
p
q
r
s
t
u
v
w
x
y
z

a
b
c
d
e
f
g
h
i
j
k
l
m
n

Oo

p
q
r
s
t
u
v
w
x
y
z

oil oils
Oil is a smooth, thick liquid. One kind of **oil** is burned to keep people warm or used in machines. Another kind of **oil** is used for cooking food.

old older, oldest
An **old** person was born a long time ago. Something **old** was made a long time ago.

once
1 If something happens **once**, it happens one time only.
2 If something happens at **once**, it happens straight away.

onion onions
An **onion** is a white vegetable with a strong taste.

only
Only means one or no more than.
*You can **only** have one chocolate.*
*Gary's little – he's **only** three.*
*This is the **only** box I can find.*

open opens, opening, opened
1 When something is **open**, it is no longer closed.
2 If you **open** something, you make it **open**.
*Dad **opened** the door.*

operation operations
When doctors repair a person's body, they do an **operation**.

opposite opposites
The **opposite** of something is different from it in every way.
*Light is the **opposite** of dark.*

orange oranges
1 An **orange** is a round, juicy fruit. It has a thick **orange** skin.

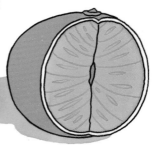

2 Orange is a colour made from a mixture of red and yellow. (See page 184.)

orchestra orchestras
An **orchestra** is a large group of people who play musical instruments together.

order orders, ordering, ordered
1 The **order** of things is how they are arranged.
The words in this book are in alphabetical order.
2 If you **order** something in a restaurant, you say you would like it.
3 If you are **ordered** to do something, you must do it.

ordinary
Ordinary means not special in any way.
*It was a very **ordinary** day. Nothing different happened.*

other
Other means not this one.
*Take your bag in this hand and hold the rail with the **other**.*

otter otters
An **otter** is a furry long-tailed animal. It lives near water. **Otters** swim well and eat fish.

our
Our means belonging to us.
*This is **our** car.*

out
1 If you go **out**, you are away from home.
*We went **out** for a meal.*
2 If a light or fire goes **out**, it stops burning.

outside
1 The **outside** of something is the part around the rest of it.
2 If you are **outside**, you are not in a building.

oval ovals
An **oval** is a flat shape with a curved edge. It is like the shape of an egg.

oven ovens
An **oven** is the cupboard in a cooker where you bake food.

over
When something is **over**, it is finished.
*When the game was **over** we all went home.*

owe owes, owing, owed
If you **owe** someone money, you have not paid them for something or you have not paid back what they lent you.

owl owls
An **owl** is a bird that usually hunts at night. It has large eyes to help it to see in the dark.

own owns, owning, owned
1 If you **own** something, it belongs to you.
2 If you are on your **own**, you are alone.

a b c d e f g h i j k l m n **Oo** p q r s t u v w x y z

a b c d e f g h i j k l m n o **Pp** q r s t u v w x y z

pack **packs, packing, packed**
When you **pack** a case or container, you put things in it.
*Masud **packed** his bags and went on holiday.*

packet **packets**
A **packet** is a small container made of paper or cardboard. Breakfast cereals and sugar come in **packets**.

paddle **paddles, paddling, paddled**
When you **paddle**, you walk in water which is not very deep.

page **pages**
A **page** is one side of a piece of paper in a book, magazine or newspaper.
*This is **page** 104 of this dictionary.*

paid See **pay**.

pain **pains**
You feel a **pain** when part of your body hurts.

paint **paints, painting, painted**
1 **Paint** is a liquid that you use to change the colour of something.
2 You can **paint** walls or pictures.

painting **paintings**
A **painting** is a picture that someone has painted.

pair **pairs**
1 Two things that go together make a **pair**. Shoes, feet and eyes all come in **pairs**.
2 Something that has two similar parts joined together can also be a **pair**.
*I want a **pair** of shoes to go with this **pair** of trousers.*

palace **palaces**
A **palace** is a very large house. Kings, queens and other important people live in **palaces**.

pale **paler, palest**
If a colour is **pale**, it is almost white.

palm **palms**
1 Your **palm** is the inside part of your hand. (See page 174.)

2 A **palm** tree grows in hot countries. It has large leaves but no branches.

pan pans

A **pan** is a round, metal container with a long handle. It is used for cooking things on top of a cooker.

pancake pancakes

A **pancake** is a very thin, flat cake. It is cooked in a flat pan.

panda pandas

A **panda** is a large black and white animal. It looks like a bear and lives in China.

panic panics, panicking, panicked

1 **Panic** is a sudden feeling of fear.
2 If you **panic**, you feel so afraid that you cannot think properly.

pantomime pantomimes

A **pantomime** is a kind of play that children see at Christmas time. It tells a fairy story and has songs and jokes.

pants

You wear **pants** under your trousers or skirt.

paper papers

1 **Paper** is a thin material. You write on **paper** and wrap parcels with it. Books are printed on **paper**.
2 **Paper** is also short for newspaper.

parcel parcels

You wrap something in a **parcel** to send it in the post or give it as a present.

parent parents

Your **parents** are your mother and your father.

park parks, parking, parked

1 A **park** is a large open space with grass and trees. People walk and play in **parks**.
2 When someone **parks** a car, they leave it for a short time.

parrot parrots

A **parrot** is a brightly coloured bird with a curved beak. Some **parrots** copy human speech.

part parts

A **part** is anything that belongs to something bigger.
*Your eyes, nose and mouth are **parts** of your face.*

party parties

A **party** is a group of people having fun together.

pass passes, passing, passed

1 When you **pass** something, you go by it without stopping.
2 When you **pass** something to someone, you give it to them.
3 If you **pass** a test, you do well.

a
b
c
d
e
f
g
h
i
j
k
l
m
n
o
Pp
q
r
s
t
u
v
w
x
y
z

105

a
b
c
d
e
f
g
h
i
j
k
l
m
n
o
Pp
q
r
s
t
u
v
w
x
y
z

passenger passengers
A **passenger** travels in a car, bus, train, aeroplane or ship.

passport passports
A **passport** is a small book that you carry when you travel to another country.

past
The **past** is the time before now.
*One minute ago, ten years ago and thousands of years ago are all in the **past**.*

pasta
Pasta is a food that you eat with sauce. Spaghetti, macaroni and noodles are all different types of **pasta**.

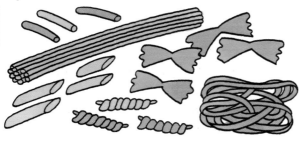

paste pastes, pasting, pasted
1 Paste is a kind of glue. It is used for sticking paper onto things.
2 If you **paste** something, you stick it with glue or **paste**.

pastry
Pastry is a mixture of flour, fat and water. It is rolled flat and baked. Tarts and pies are made with **pastry**.

pat pats, patting, patted
When you **pat** something, you touch it gently with the palm of your hand.
*Carlos **patted** the dog on the head.*

path paths
A **path** is like a small lane for people to walk along.
*We took the **path** through the forest.*

patient patients
1 A **patient** is an ill person who is being looked after.
2 A **patient** person stays calm when things go wrong.
*Please be **patient** – dinner's a bit late today.*

pattern patterns
1 A **pattern** is a set of repeated marks.

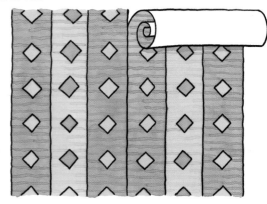

2 A **pattern** is also the way that numbers or letters are related to one another.
*Find the **pattern** in these numbers: 2, 4, 6, 8.*

pavement pavements
A **pavement** is a hard path at the side of a road.
*Don't walk in the road! Stay on the **pavement**.*

paw paws
A **paw** is the foot of an animal such as a cat or a bear.

pay pays, paying, paid
If you **pay** for something, you give money for it.

PC PCs
A **PC** is a computer that is used by one or two people at a time. **PC** is short for personal computer.

pea peas
A **pea** is a small, round, green vegetable. **Peas** grow in long, green shells called pods.

peace
Peace is a quiet time, when no one is fighting.

peach peaches
A **peach** is a round, soft, juicy fruit. It has a large stone and a furry skin.

peacock peacocks
A **peacock** is a large, blue and green male bird. It can open its tail like a fan. The female is called a peahen.

peanut peanuts
A **peanut** is a small nut. It grows in a shell under the ground.

pear pears
A **pear** is a juicy fruit that grows on a tree.

pebble pebbles
A **pebble** is a small, round stone.

peck pecks, pecking, pecked
When a bird **pecks**, it bites at something quickly with its beak.

pedal pedals, pedalling, pedalled
1 A **pedal** is part of a bike. (See page 175.)
2 When you **pedal** a bike, you push the **pedals** with your feet.

peel peels, peeling, peeled
1 **Peel** is the skin of some fruit and vegetables.
2 When you **peel** something, you take off its skin.

peg pegs
You use a **peg** when you hang something up.
*Mum uses clothes **pegs** to hang the washing on the line.*

pen pens
You use a **pen** when you write or draw with ink.
*I drew this picture with a **pen**.*

pence See **penny**.

pencil pencils
A **pencil** is a thin stick of wood with a grey or coloured centre. You use a **pencil** to write or draw.

a
b
c
d
e
f
g
h
i
j
k
l
m
n
o
Pp
q
r
s
t
u
v
w
x
y
z

107

a
b
c
d
e
f
g
h
i
j
k
l
m
n
o
Pp
q
r
s
t
u
v
w
x
y
z

penguin penguins

A **penguin** is a large black and white bird that lives where it is very cold. It cannot fly but uses its wings for swimming.

penny pence or pennies

A **penny** is a British coin. There are 100 **pence** in a pound. The symbol for **pence** is p.

pentagon pentagons

A **pentagon** is a flat shape that has five sides. (See page 184.)

people

People means more than one person. See **person**.

pepper peppers

1 Pepper is a powder with a hot taste used to flavour food.

2 A **pepper** is a hollow red, green or yellow vegetable. It sometimes tastes hot and spicy.

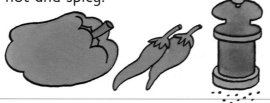

perform performs, performing, performed

1 When you **perform**, you do something in front of an audience.
*The magician **performed** his magic tricks on the stage.*

2 When you **perform** an action, you do it.

period periods

A **period** of time has a beginning and an end.
*The rain fell for short **periods** of time.*

person people

A **person** is a man, woman or child. A **person** can also be called a human.

pest pests

A **pest** is an insect or small animal that damages plants and crops.

pet pets

A **pet** is an animal that you look after. **Pets** often live in your home.
*We keep a dog, a cat and a pony as **pets**.*

petal petals

A **petal** is a coloured part of a flower.

petrol

People put **petrol** in a car to make the engine work.

phone phones

You use a **phone** to speak to someone in another place. **Phone** is short for telephone.

photograph photographs, photographing, photographed

1 A **photograph,** or **photo**, is a picture made using a camera and film.

2 If you **photograph** something, you take a **photo** of it.

piano pianos

A **piano** is a large musical instrument. You press black and white keys to make music.

pick picks, picking, picked

1 When you **pick** something, you choose it.

2 If you **pick** a flower, you take it off its plant.

3 When you **pick** something up, you lift it.

picnic picnics

If you have a **picnic**, you carry a meal somewhere and eat it outside.
*We took a **picnic** to the beach.*

pictogram pictograms

A **pictogram** is a kind of graph. It uses pictures instead of lines.

picture pictures

A **picture** is a drawing, painting or photograph.

pie pies

A **pie** is fruit, meat or other food covered in pastry and baked in the oven.

piece pieces

A **piece** of something is a part of it.
*Mum gave me a **piece** of apple pie.*

pier piers

A **pier** is a long platform built out into the sea.

pig pigs

A **pig** is a farm animal. It has a snout and a curly tail. The meat from a **pig** is called pork.

pigeon pigeons

A **pigeon** is a bird that is often seen in towns and cities.

pile piles

A **pile** is a number of things put on top of one another.
*Please put your clothes in a neat **pile**.*

pill pills

A **pill** is a kind of medicine. It is small and round so that it can be swallowed without chewing.

pillow pillows

A **pillow** is a bag filled with soft material. You rest your head on a **pillow** when you are in bed.

pilot pilots

A **pilot** flies an aeroplane.

a
b
c
d
e
f
g
h
i
j
k
l
m
n
o
Pp
q
r
s
t
u
v
w
x
y
z

a
b
c
d
e
f
g
h
i
j
k
l
m
n
o

Pp

q
r
s
t
u
v
w
x
y
z

pin pins
A **pin** is a short, thin piece of metal with a sharp point. You use **pins** to hold pieces of cloth together.

pineapple pineapples
A **pineapple** is a large fruit with sweet, juicy yellow flesh. It has a thick, lumpy brown skin and grows in hot countries.

pint pints
Liquids like milk can be measured in **pints**.

pipe pipes
A **pipe** is a long tube. **Pipes** carry liquids or gas from one place to another.

pirate pirates
A **pirate** is a sailor who attacks and robs other ships.

pizza pizzas
A **pizza** is a round, flat piece of bread covered with cheese, tomatoes and other foods. It is baked in a very hot oven.

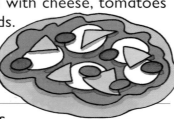

place places
1 A **place** is a piece of land or a building.
2 A **place** is where something or someone is.
*Don't move – stay in your **places**!*
3 The number 542 has a 5 in the hundreds **place**, a 4 in the tens **place** and a 2 in the units **place**.

plain plainer, plainest
Plain means simple or without decoration.
*Emma wore a **plain** green top.*

plan plans, planning, planned
1 If you **plan** something, you decide how to do it.
2 A **plan** is a drawing or diagram of something that is to be made.

plane planes
A **plane** is a large flying vehicle that carries people or things. It has wings and one or more engines. **Plane** is short for aeroplane.

planet planets
A **planet** is a large, round object in space that moves around a star. Earth is a **planet** that travels around the Sun once a year. Some **planets** have rings.

plant plants, planting, planted
1 A **plant** is anything that lives that is not an animal. Trees and flowers are **plants**. Mushrooms and grass are **plants**, too.
2 If you **plant** something, you put seeds or **plants** into the ground to grow.
*We've **planted** some poppy seeds in the garden.*

plaster plasters

1 A **plaster** is a strip of material that you stick on when you cut yourself.

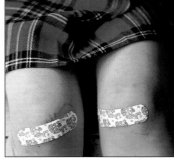

2 Plaster is also a soft, white mixture that goes hard when it dries. **Plaster** is spread on walls to make them smooth.

plastic plastics

Plastic is a strong, light material made in factories. It is used for buckets, bottles, plates, toys and many other things.

plate plates

A **plate** is a flat dish that you put food on.

platform platforms

1 You stand on a **platform** so that you can be seen easily. It is higher than the rest of the room.
2 You stand on a **platform** at a railway station to wait for a train.

play plays, playing, played

1 When you **play** a game, you do something for fun.
2 If you **play** a musical instrument, you make music with it.
3 A **play** is a story that is performed by actors.

playground playgrounds

A **playground** is a place outside where children play.

playtime

Playtime is when you come out of the classroom to play.

please pleases, pleasing, pleased

1 If you **please** someone, you make them happy.
2 You say **please** when you ask for something.
Please may I have an ice cream?

plenty

If there is **plenty** of something, there is a lot of it.
*Help yourself – there's **plenty** of food!*

plough ploughs

A **plough** is a farm tool. It cuts up the earth so that seeds can be planted.

plum plums

A **plum** is a small, juicy red or yellow fruit. It has a smooth skin and a stone in the middle.

plump plumper, plumpest

If someone or something is **plump**, they are a bit fat.
*Our cat is **plump** and cuddly.*

plural plurals

Plural means more than one. Many **plural** words end in the letter s.
*"Dogs" is the **plural** of "dog".*
*"Children" is the **plural** of "child".*

a
b
c
d
e
f
g
h
i
j
k
l
m
n
o
Pp
q
r
s
t
u
v
w
x
y
z

a
b
c
d
e
f
g
h
i
j
k
l
m
n
o

Pp

q
r
s
t
u
v
w
x
y
z

plus

Plus is another word you can use when you add. The symbol + means **plus**.

pocket pockets

A **pocket** is a small bag sewn into clothes. You keep things in your **pockets**.

poem poems

A **poem** is a piece of writing that uses language in a special way. It uses rhythm and often rhyme.

poet poets

A **poet** is a person who writes poems.

poetry

Poetry means poems or a collection of poems.

point points, pointing, pointed

1 If you **point** at something, you hold your finger towards it to show where it is.
2 The **point** of something is the sharp part at the end.

pointed

Something **pointed** has a sharp point at the end.

poisonous

If something is **poisonous**, it makes you ill if you eat or drink it.
*Some mushrooms are **poisonous**.*

polar bear polar bears

A **polar bear** is a large white bear. It lives near the North Pole.

pole poles

1 A **pole** is a long, thin piece of wood or metal.
*The tent was held up by metal **poles**.*
2 The North **Pole** and the South **Pole** are places at opposite ends of the Earth.
*The **Poles** are covered in ice and are the coldest places on Earth.*

police

The **police** are men and women who make sure that no one breaks the law. They are often called **policemen**, **policewomen** or **police officers**.
*The **police** are looking for the burglars.*

polish polishes, polishing, polished

If you **polish** something, you rub it to make it shine. You often use a cloth with **polish** on it.

polite

A **polite** person behaves well and is not rude.
*It is **polite** to hold the door open for other people.*

pond ponds

A **pond** is a small area of water in a garden or field.

pony ponies

A **pony** is a small horse.

pool pools

1 A **pool** is a small area of still water next to the sea.

Paul and Martha found lots of little crabs in the rock pool.

2 Pool is also short for swimming **pool**.

poor poorer, poorest

A **poor** person does not have very much money.

pop pops, popping, popped

1 If you **pop** a balloon, it bursts with a short, sharp sound.

2 Pop is modern popular music.

popcorn

You eat **popcorn** as a snack with salt or sugar. Seeds of corn are heated until they burst.

poppy poppies

A **poppy** is a wild plant. It has a large red flower.

popular

If something is **popular**, lots of people like it.

porridge

Porridge is a hot breakfast cereal. It is made from oats and water or milk.

position positions

1 Your **position** is where you are or how your body is arranged.

2 Your **position** is also where you play in a team.

"What position do you play?" "I'm the goalkeeper."

possible

If something is **possible**, it can be done or can happen.

It's still possible to get tickets for the match.

post posts, posting, posted

1 The **post** is the letters that come to your house.

2 When you **post** a letter, you put it in a postbox.

3 A **post** is a piece of wood or metal fixed upright in the ground.

poster posters

A **poster** is a large notice or picture. It is put up to tell people about something.

Did you see the poster on the wall about the pantomime?

postman postmen

A **postman** collects and delivers letters and parcels.

a
b
c
d
e
f
g
h
i
j
k
l
m
n
o
Pp
q
r
s
t
u
v
w
x
y
z

post office **post offices**
A **post office** is a shop where you can send letters and parcels. It also sells stamps.

pot **pots**
A **pot** is a round container. **Pots** hold many different things, and some are used for cooking food.

potato **potatoes**
A **potato** is a common vegetable. It grows under the ground. Chips and crisps are made from **potatoes**.

pound **pounds**
British money is measured in **pounds** and pence. The symbol for **pound** is £.

pour **pours, pouring, poured**
1 If you **pour** a liquid, you tip it out of its container.
2 When it is **pouring** with rain, it is raining heavily.

powder
Powder is a solid material that is in very tiny pieces. Flour is a **powder**.

power
The **power** of something is its strength.
*A lorry's engine has more **power** than a car's engine.*

practice **practices**
Practice means doing something many times to get better at it.
*Try to get lots of spelling **practice** before the test.*

practise **practises, practising, practised**
If you **practise** something, you do it many times to get better at it.
*I am **practising** my song for the show.*

pram **prams**
You can push a baby from place to place in a **pram**.

pray **prays, praying, prayed**
If you **pray**, you talk to your god.

predict **predicts, predicting, predicted**
If you **predict** something, you say it will happen in the future.

present **presents**
1 You give people **presents** on their birthday or at Christmas.
2 The **present** is now.
3 If you are **present** somewhere, you are there.

press **presses, pressing, pressed**
When you **press** something, you push hard on it.
*Mick **pressed** the doorbell.*

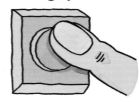

pretend pretends, pretending, pretended
If you **pretend**, you try to be something you are not.
*Let's **pretend** to be pirates. This tree can be our ship.*

pretty prettier, prettiest
Pretty means nice to look at.
*Those kittens are really **pretty**!*

price prices
The **price** of something is the money you pay for it.

prick pricks, pricking, pricked
If you **prick** something, you make a tiny hole using a sharp point.

prince princes
A **prince** is the son of a king or queen.

princess princesses
1 The daughter of a king or queen is called a **princess**.
2 The wife of a prince is sometimes called a **princess**.

print prints, printing, printed
When words and pictures are **printed**, they are put on the paper using a machine. Usually lots of copies are **printed** at once.
*The pages of this dictionary are **printed**.*

printer printers
1 A **printer** prints books or newspapers using a machine.
2 A **printer** is also a machine that prints information from a computer.

prison prisons
People who have broken the law sometimes go to **prison**.

prize prizes
You win a **prize** if you are very good at something or by being lucky.

problem problems
A **problem** is something that is hard to sort out.
*I've got a **problem** – my lace is broken.*

program programs
A **program** is a set of instructions that tell a computer what to do.

programme programmes
1 A **programme** is a show on television or radio.
2 A **programme** is a small book of information about a show or a sports match.

project projects
If you are doing a **project**, you find lots of information about something and then write about it.
*I did a **project** on dinosaurs at school.*

a b c d e f g h i j k l m n o **Pp** q r s t u v w x y z

a
b
c
d
e
f
g
h
i
j
k
l
m
n
o

Pp

q
r
s
t
u
v
w
x
y
z

promise promises, promising, promised

If you **promise** to do something, you mean that you really will do it.

*Mum **promised** that we'd go to the swings today.*

pronoun pronouns

A **pronoun** is a word like "me" or "your". It is used instead of a noun. (See page 179.)

proper

Proper means right or correct.

*Put those books back in their **proper** place, please.*

protect protects, protecting, protected

If you **protect** someone or something, you keep them safe.

*Ruby wore a helmet to **protect** her head when she rode her bike.*

proud prouder, proudest

When you are **proud** of someone, you feel very pleased with them because they have done well.

*This school is very **proud** of the winning netball team.*

prove proves, proving, proved

When you **prove** something, you show that it is true.

*I can **prove** Neil wasn't there because he was at my house!*

publisher publishers

A **publisher** prints and sells books, newspapers or magazines.

pudding puddings

A **pudding** is a sweet food that you eat at the end of a meal.

puddle puddles

A **puddle** is a small pool of water that is left after rain.

pull pulls, pulling, pulled

When you **pull** something, you hold it and make it come towards you.

pumpkin pumpkins

A **pumpkin** is a large, round, orange vegetable. People make **pumpkin** lanterns at Halloween.

punctuation

Punctuation means signs like full stops, commas and question marks. Here are some **punctuation** marks: . , " " ' ! ?

puncture punctures

A **puncture** is a small hole made by something sharp. If a tyre has a **puncture**, the air gets out and it goes flat.

*Dad mended the **puncture** in my tyre.*

punish punishes, punishing, punished

If someone is **punished**, they are made unhappy because they have done something wrong.
*Mum **punished** Jenny for being rude by sending her to her room.*

punishment punishments

A **punishment** is something unpleasant that happens to someone who has done wrong.

pupil pupils

1 The **pupils** at school are the children who go there to learn.
2 The **pupil** of your eye is the black part in the middle.

puppet puppets

A **puppet** is a small toy figure of a person or animal. You move a **puppet** by pulling strings or by putting your hand inside its body.

puppy puppies

A **puppy** is a young dog.

pure purer, purest

Something that is **pure** has nothing else mixed with it.

purse purses

You keep money in a **purse**.

push pushes, pushing, pushed

If you **push** something, you move it away from you with your hands.

pushchair pushchairs

A **pushchair** is a small folding chair on wheels. Little children are taken around in **pushchairs**.

put puts, putting, put

When you **put** something somewhere, you place it there.
*I **put** my book in my bag.*

puzzle puzzles

A **puzzle** is something that is hard to understand or work out. People do **puzzles** for fun.
*I enjoyed doing the crossword **puzzle**.*

pyjamas

Pyjamas are a loose top and trousers that you wear in bed.

pyramid pyramids

1 A **pyramid** is a solid shape. Its sides are triangles that meet in a point at the top.
2 The **Pyramids** are huge stone buildings in Egypt.

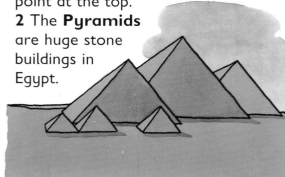

a
b
c
d
e
f
g
h
i
j
k
l
m
n
o
Pp
q
r
s
t
u
v
w
x
y
z

a b c d e f g h i j k l m n o p **Qq** r s t u v w x y z

quack quacks

A **quack** is the cry of a duck. It is a loud, hard sound.

quarrel quarrels, quarrelling, quarrelled

1 A **quarrel** is an angry argument.
2 When you **quarrel** with someone, you talk angrily to each other.
My sister and I quarrelled about who should clean out the rabbit hutch.

quarter quarters

1 When you divide something exactly into four, each piece is a **quarter**.

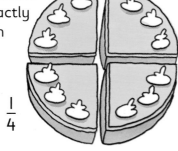

$\frac{1}{4}$

2 Quarter past ten means 15 minutes after ten o'clock. **Quarter** to ten means 15 minutes before ten o'clock.

queen queens

1 A **queen** is a woman who rules a country because she belongs to a royal family.
2 The wife of a king is also called a **queen**.

question questions

When you ask a **question**, you want to know something.
Who can answer Alice's question about the homework?

question mark question marks

A **question mark** is used at the end of a sentence that asks a question.

Does this sentence need a question mark? Is it asking a question?

queue queues

When you are in a **queue**, you are standing in a line of people waiting for something.
There was a queue outside the cinema.

quick quicker, quickest

Something **quick** does not take long.
Can I have a quick look at your book?

quickly

If you do something **quickly**, you do it in very little time.

quiet quieter, quietest

When someone is **quiet**, they make very little noise.

quite

1 Quite means more than a bit.
I am quite hungry but not starving.
2 Not **quite** means nearly.
I have not quite finished my writing.

quiz quizzes

A **quiz** is a kind of game. People are asked questions to find out who knows most.

Rr

rabbit rabbits

A **rabbit** is a small furry animal with long ears. Wild **rabbits** live in tunnels under the ground.

race races

A **race** is a competition to see who is the fastest.
My friend won the sack race.

radiator radiators

A **radiator** is a metal container filled with liquid. It is used to heat a room.

radio radios

A **radio** turns waves in the air into programmes that you can hear.
I listen to music on my radio.

raft rafts

A **raft** is a flat boat. It is made from long pieces of wood joined together.

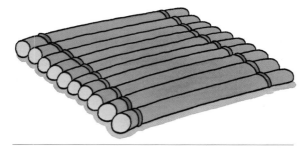

rag rags

A **rag** is a piece of old cloth. **Rags** are used to clean or wipe things.

railway railways

A **railway** is the metal bars that trains run along.

rain rains, raining, rained

When it **rains**, little drops of water called **rain** fall from the sky.

rainbow rainbows

A **rainbow** is a band of different colours in the sky. You sometimes see a **rainbow** when the sun shines through rain. The colours of the **rainbow** are red, orange, yellow, green, blue, indigo and violet.

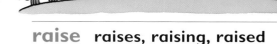

raise raises, raising, raised

1 If you **raise** something, you lift it up higher.
2 If you **raise** your voice, you speak louder.

rake rakes

A **rake** is a garden tool used for collecting leaves and grass into piles. It has a row of metal teeth and a long handle.

Ramadan

Ramadan is a time when Muslims do not eat or drink during daylight hours.

ran See **run**.

a
b
c
d
e
f
g
h
i
j
k
l
m
n
o
p
q
Rr
s
t
u
v
w
x
y
z

a
b
c
d
e
f
g
h
i
j
k
l
m
n
o
p
q
Rr
s
t
u
v
w
x
y
z

rang See **ring**.

rare **rarer, rarest**
Something that is **rare** is not seen very often.
This is a rare bird – there are only fifty in the whole world.

raspberry **raspberries**
A **raspberry** is a small, soft, red fruit.

rat **rats**
A **rat** is an animal that looks like a large mouse. It has sharp teeth and a long tail.

rather
1 If you would **rather** do something, you would like to do it more than something else.
I'd rather stay in than go out.
2 If something is **rather** cold, it is a bit cold.

rattle **rattles, rattling, rattled**
1 When something **rattles**, it makes short, quick, knocking sounds.
2 A **rattle** is a toy which a baby shakes to make a noise.

raw
Raw food is not cooked.
Raw carrots are sweet and crisp.

reach **reaches, reaching, reached**
1 When you **reach** a place, you arrive there.
2 When you **reach** for something, you stretch out your hand towards it.
I reached for a book on the top shelf.

read **reads, reading, read**
1 When you can turn written letters into words and sentences, you can **read**.
2 When you **read** aloud, you say the words that are written.
I am reading a bedtime story.

ready
If you are **ready**, you can start straight away.
I've packed my bag and I'm ready to go.

real
1 If something is **real**, it is a fact or it is true.
This is a story about a real person who is still alive today.
2 A **real** thing is exactly what it is meant to be and not a copy.
This is a real diamond, not a piece of glass.

really
You use **really** to show that something is true.
Did you really see a monkey at the zoo?
I'm really tired.

rearrange **rearranges, rearranging, rearranged**
If you **rearrange** things, you put them in a different order.

reason **reasons**
A **reason** tells you why something has happened.
The reason I'm late is that the bus broke down.

receive **receives, receiving, received**
If you **receive** something, it is sent or given to you.
I received a letter from my granny.

recipe **recipes**
A **recipe** is a set of instructions. It tells you how to make something to eat or drink.

recite **recites, reciting, recited**
If you **recite** a poem, you say it out loud.

record **records, recording, recorded**
1 Someone who does something better than anybody else sets a **record**.
2 If you **record** something, you put it on tape or write it down.

recorder **recorders**
A **recorder** is a musical instrument. It is played by blowing into one end.

recount **recounts, recounting, recounted**
If you **recount** a story, you tell it.

rectangle **rectangles**
A **rectangle** is a shape with four sides and four corners that are all right angles. Its opposite sides are the same length.

rectangular
Anything in the shape of a rectangle is **rectangular**. A football pitch is **rectangular**.

reflection **reflections**
1 When you look in a mirror, you see a **reflection** of yourself.

2 A **reflection** of something is also a copy where everything is the other way round.

a
b
c
d
e
f
g
h
i
j
k
l
m
n
o
p
q

Rr

s
t
u
v
w
x
y
z

refrigerator **refrigerators**
You keep food cold and fresh in a large metal cupboard called a **refrigerator**. A **refrigerator** is often called a fridge.

refuse **refuses, refusing, refused**
If you **refuse** to do something, you say that you will not do it.
Mum asked if I would like to go shopping, but I refused.

remember **remembers, remembering, remembered**
If you **remember** something, you can bring it back to your mind.
I can remember my first day at school.

remind **reminds, reminding, reminded**
If you **remind** someone to do something, you make them remember to do it.
Liam reminded me to take my book home.

remove **removes, removing, removed**
If you **remove** something, you take it away.
Please remove your bags from the floor.

repair **repairs, repairing, repaired**
If you **repair** something that is broken, you mend it.

repeat **repeats, repeating, repeated**
When something is **repeated**, it happens all over again.
I'm going to watch that programme again when it is repeated next week.

reply **replies, replying, replied**
1 If you **reply** to something, you give an answer.
I haven't replied to Annie's invitation yet.
2 A **reply** is the answer you give.
I haven't sent a reply yet.

report **reports**
A **report** tells you the facts about something.
We read a book on goldfish and then wrote a report on how to look after them.

represent **represents, representing, represented**
A letter or symbol that takes the place of a number or word **represents** it.

reptile **reptiles**
A **reptile** is an animal with cold blood and scaly skin. **Reptiles** have short legs or no legs at all. They usually lay eggs.

rescue **rescues, rescuing, rescued**
If you **rescue** someone, you save them from danger.
The farmer rescued the cow from the river.

rest rests, resting, rested
1 When you **rest**, you are quiet and do nothing for a while.
Gran is resting in her chair.
2 You have a **rest** when you sit or lie down quietly.
Gran always has a rest after lunch.
3 The **rest** of something is all that remains of it.
I ate half the cake and couldn't finish the rest.

restaurant restaurants
You can buy and eat a meal at a **restaurant**.

result results
A **result** is what happens because something else has happened.
Alex missed his bus, and as a result was late for school.

retell retells, retelling, retold
If you **retell** a story, you tell it again in a new way.
This story has been retold all over the world.

return returns, returning, returned
1 If you **return**, you go back to the place where you were before.
Mum has just returned home from work.
2 If you **return** something to someone, you give it back to them.
I'll return Jim's book when I've read it.

reward rewards, rewarding, rewarded
You can be given a **reward** for doing something well.
The police gave Jason a reward for finding the gold watch.

rhinoceros rhinoceroses
A **rhinoceros**, or **rhino**, is a large wild animal. It has one or two horns on its nose. **Rhinoceroses** live in Africa and Asia.

rhyme rhymes, rhyming, rhymed
1 Words that **rhyme** end with the same sound, like *bean* and *green*.
2 A **rhyme** is a short rhyming poem.

rhythm rhythms
A **rhythm** is a repeated pattern of sound in music or poetry.

ribbon ribbons
A **ribbon** is a long, narrow piece of coloured material.
I put yellow ribbon around the parcel.

rice
Rice is a plant that grows in hot countries. You can cook and eat the seeds of the **rice** plant.

rich richer, richest
A **rich** person has a lot of money.

riddle riddles
A **riddle** is a difficult question with a funny answer.
Here is a riddle. What gets bigger the more you take away? A hole!

a
b
c
d
e
f
g
h
i
j
k
l
m
n
o
p
q
Rr
s
t
u
v
w
x
y
z

a
b
c
d
e
f
g
h
i
j
k
l
m
n
o
p
q
Rr
s
t
u
v
w
x
y
z

ride **rides, riding, rode, ridden**
1 If you **ride** a bike or a horse, you sit on it and control how it moves.
2 When you **ride** in a bus, car or train, you travel in it.

right
1 **Right** means the opposite of left. *Tom has his **right** foot on the ball.*
2 **Right** also means correct. *Well done! You got all your sums **right**.*
3 **Right** can also mean exactly. *Stand **right** in the middle of the circle.*

right angle **right angles**
A **right angle** is an angle of 90 degrees. The symbol for it is a small square. *The sides of a square meet at **right angles**.*

ring **rings, ringing, rang, rung**
1 A **ring** is a small circle of metal that you wear on your finger.
2 When you shake or press a bell and it makes a noise, it **rings**.

ripe **riper, ripest**
When fruit is **ripe**, it is ready to eat. *That tomato is still green because it isn't **ripe** yet.*

rise **rises, rising, rose, risen**
1 If something **rises**, it moves upwards.
2 If you **rise**, you stand up.

river **rivers**
A **river** is water that flows through the land to a sea or a lake.

road **roads**
A **road** is a long piece of hard ground. Cars and other vehicles travel along **roads**.

roar **roars**
A **roar** is a deep, loud noise like a lion makes.

robin **robins**
A **robin** is a small brown bird with a red breast.

robot **robots**
A **robot** is a machine controlled by a computer. **Robots** can move and do jobs that people usually do. *A lot of cars are made by **robots**.*

rock **rocks, rocking, rocked**
1 **Rock** is the very hard material that the surface of the Earth is made of. Pieces of this are called **rocks**.
2 If you **rock** something, you move it gently from side to side.

rocket **rockets**
1 A **rocket** is a vehicle shaped like a pointed tube that goes into space.
2 A **rocket** is also a firework that explodes high up in the sky.

rod **rods**
A **rod** is a long, thin piece of wood or metal. **Rods** are used for fishing.

rode See **ride**.

roll **rolls, rolling, rolled**
1 When an object such as a wheel moves across a surface, it **rolls**.
2 A **roll** of something is a long piece wrapped round and round on itself. Sticky tape comes on a **roll**.
3 A bread **roll** is a small, round piece of bread.

roof **roofs**
The **roof** of a building or car is the top part of it.

room **rooms**
A **room** is part of a building. It has its own walls, floor and ceiling.

root **roots**
A **root** is the part of a plant that grows under the ground.

rope **ropes**
Rope is a very thick, strong type of string. It is made by twisting together many threads.

rose **roses**
A **rose** is a beautiful garden flower with a lovely smell.

rough **rougher, roughest**
1 If something is **rough**, it is bumpy and not smooth.
2 **Rough** weather is stormy and not quiet.

roughly
Roughly means about but not exactly.
*I'll be there at **roughly** five o'clock.*

round
Something **round** has a shape like a circle or a ball.

roundabout **roundabouts**
1 Where roads cross, you often find a **roundabout**. Vehicles go around the **roundabout** until they reach the road they want.
2 A **roundabout** is a ride at a fair.

route **routes**
Your **route** is how you get from one place to another.
*There are two **routes** from here to my house.*

row **rows, rowing, rowed**
1 (*sounds like* toe) A **row** is a line of things or people side by side.
2 (*sounds like* toe) When you **row** a boat, you move it through the water using oars.

3 (*sounds like* cow) When people are angry and shout at each other, they are having a **row**.

a b c d e f g h i j k l m n o p q **Rr** s t u v w x y z

a b c d e f g h i j k l m n o p q **Rr** s t u v w x y z

royal

Queens, kings and members of their family are **royal**. They are all members of the **royal** family.

rub rubs, rubbing, rubbed

1 If you **rub** something, you move your hand, or something you are holding, backwards and forwards across it.
*I **rubbed** my shoes until they shone.*
2 If you **rub** something out, you make it disappear by **rubbing** it.
*I **rubbed** out my writing and started again.*

rubber rubbers

1 Rubber is a strong, stretchy material. Car tyres and wellington boots are made of **rubber**.
2 You use a **rubber** to get rid of pencil marks on paper.

rubbish

Rubbish is the things that you throw away.

ruby rubies

A **ruby** is a red jewel.

rude ruder, rudest

A **rude** person behaves badly and is not polite.
*It is **rude** to call people names!*

rug rugs

1 A **rug** is a small, thick carpet.
2 A **rug** is also a blanket which you can sit on outdoors or wrap around you to keep warm.

ruin ruins, ruining, ruined

1 If you **ruin** something, you spoil it completely.
*The rain **ruined** our holiday.*
2 A **ruin** is a building that is almost completely destroyed.

rule rules, ruling, ruled

1 A **rule** describes what you must do or what always happens.
*Eating in the library is against the **rules**.*
2 Someone who **rules** a country tells everybody else what to do.

ruler rulers

1 A **ruler** is used for measuring or for drawing straight lines.

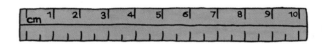

2 A **ruler** is also someone who rules a country.

run runs, running, ran, run

1 When you **run**, you move quickly and both your feet come off the ground at once.
2 If you **run** a bath, you turn on the taps and fill it up.
3 A **run** is a point in cricket or baseball.

rung See **ring**.

rush rushes, rushing, rushed

1 If you **rush**, you do something or go somewhere very quickly.
*We **rushed** to the shops before they closed.*
2 If you are in a **rush**, you are busy and do not have enough time to do things.

Ss

sack sacks

A **sack** is a large bag. It is made of cloth or plastic and used to carry or store things in.

*The **sack** of potatoes was heavy.*

sad sadder, saddest

If you are **sad**, you do not feel happy.

*I was very **sad** when we left our old house.*

saddle saddles

You sit on a **saddle** when you ride a horse or a bicycle.

safe safer, safest; safes

1 If someone or something is **safe**, they are not in danger.

*Lock your bike in the garage. It will be **safe** there.*

2 A **safe** is a strong metal box with special locks. You can keep money and valuable things in a **safe**.

said See **say**.

sail sails, sailing, sailed

1 A **sail** is a large piece of cloth fixed onto a boat. The boat is moved through the water by the wind blowing into the **sails**.

2 If you **sail**, you travel in a boat.

*We are **sailing** on the four o'clock ferry.*

sailor sailors

A **sailor** works on a ship.

salad salads

Salad is a mixture of raw vegetables and other things, eaten cold.

sale sales

During a **sale**, shops sell things at lower prices.

*Mum bought my coat for half price in the **sale**.*

salt

Salt is a white powder that is used to flavour food. **Salt** is found in the ground and in sea water.

same

1 If two things are the **same**, they are exactly like each other.

2 If things happen at the **same** time, they happen together exactly.

sand

Sand is a powder made from very tiny bits of rock. **Sand** is found on beaches and in deserts.

sandal sandals

A **sandal** is a light, open shoe that you wear in warm weather.

a
b
c
d
e
f
g
h
i
j
k
l
m
n
o
p
q
r
Ss
t
u
v
w
x
y
z

127

a b c d e f g h i j k l m n o p q r **Ss** t u v w x y z

sandpit sandpits
A **sandpit** is a box filled with sand for children to dig in.

sandwich sandwiches
You make a **sandwich** by putting a filling between two pieces of bread.

sang See **sing**.

sank See **sink**.

sari saris
A **sari** is a piece of of clothing worn by Indian women. It is a long piece of material folded around the body in a special way.

sat See **sit**.

satellite satellites
A **satellite** is something that is sent into space to travel round and round the Earth. **Satellites** send back new information or pass signals from one part of the Earth to another.
*The television pictures came from Australia by **satellite**.*

Saturday Saturdays
Saturday is the day of the week between Friday and Sunday.

sauce sauces
A **sauce** is a thick, cooked liquid. It is served with food to give it more flavour.
*My favourite meal is fish fingers, chips and peas covered in tomato **sauce**.*

saucepan saucepans
A **saucepan** is a deep metal pot with a long handle and a lid. You cook food in a **saucepan**.

saucer saucers
A **saucer** is a small, round plate that you put a cup on.

sausage sausages
A **sausage** is made from very tiny pieces of meat put into a skin.

save saves, saving, saved
1 If you **save** someone, you stop them from being hurt or killed.
*My mum **saved** me from drowning.*
2 If you **save** your money, you keep it so that you can spend it later.

saw saws
1 A **saw** is a tool for cutting wood. It has a blade with sharp teeth.
2 *I **saw** a puppy at the park.* See **see**.

say says, saying, said
When you **say** something, you make words with your voice.

scale scales
1 You weigh something using a set of **scales.**
2 A fish is covered in **scales**. A **scale** is a piece of hard skin.

scare **scares, scaring, scared**
If something **scares** you, you feel frightened.

scared
When you are **scared,** you are afraid.
Our dog is scared of fireworks.

scarf **scarfs or scarves**
A **scarf** is a long piece of material. You wear it around your neck to keep you warm.

scent **scents**
The **scent** of something is what it smells like.

school **schools**
Children go to **school** to learn.

science **sciences**
When you learn about **science**, you find out about plants and animals. You also learn about materials like water and metal, and things like sound, light and electricity.

scissors
You use **scissors** to cut paper or cloth. They have two sharp blades and handles with holes for your fingers.

score **scores, scoring, scored**
1 You **score** a goal at football by putting the ball into the net.
2 The number of points the teams have in a match is called the **score**.

scratch **scratches, scratching, scratched**
1 If you **scratch** something, you make marks with something sharp.
The cat scratched the table with her claws.
2 A **scratch** is a mark or small cut.

scream **screams, screaming, screamed**
If you **scream**, you give a loud high shout because you are frightened or excited.

screech **screeches, screeching, screeched**
When something **screeches**, it makes a loud, high noise.
The brakes screeched as the car came to a sudden stop.

screen **screens**
A **screen** is the part of a television or computer where the pictures or writing appear.

screw **screws, screwing, screwed**
1 A **screw** is a thin, pointed piece of metal. It looks like a nail but you put it in by turning it round and round.
2 If you **screw** things together, you fix them together using **screws**.

sea **seas**
The **sea** is the salty water that covers most of the Earth's surface.

a
b
c
d
e
f
g
h
i
j
k
l
m
n
o
p
q
r
Ss
t
u
v
w
x
y
z

a
b
c
d
e
f
g
h
i
j
k
l
m
n
o
p
q
r

Ss

t
u
v
w
x
y
z

seal seals
A **seal** is an animal with short fur. **Seals** live in the sea and on land.

search searches, searching, searched
If you **search** for something, you look carefully for it.
I've searched everywhere for my watch but I can't find it!

seaside
The **seaside** is any place beside the sea.

season seasons
The year is divided into four parts called **seasons**. The four **seasons** are called spring, summer, autumn and winter.

seat seats
A **seat** is somewhere that you sit.

second seconds
1 A **second** is a small amount of time. There are 60 **seconds** in a minute.
2 The **second** in a list of things comes just after the first.

secret secrets
A **secret** is something that only a few people know about.
Mum's birthday party is a secret.

see sees, seeing, saw, seen
1 When you **see** something, your eyes notice it.
2 If you go to **see** someone, you visit them.

seed seeds
A **seed** is a small, hard object in the fruit of a plant. When it is ripe, it can grow in the ground into a new plant.

seek seeks, seeking, sought
If you **seek** something, you look for it.
The pirate was seeking the buried treasure.

seem seems, seeming, seemed
If something **seems** to be true, it looks as if it is true.
Bronwen seems shy, but she's not.
The cat seems to be hungry.

seen See **see**.

seesaw seesaws
A **seesaw** is an outdoor toy. One child sits at each end of a long piece of wood. They go up and down in turn.

selfish
Selfish people only care about themselves.

sell **sells, selling, sold**
When you **sell** something, you give it to someone who pays you money for it.

semicircle **semicircles**
A **semicircle** is exactly half a circle.

send **sends, sending, sent**
When you **send** something to a place, you make it go there.
*Mum **sent** me upstairs to wash my hands.*

sense **senses**
People have five **senses**. They can hear, see, taste, feel and smell.

sensible
Sensible people are good at knowing what is the best thing to do.

sent See **send**.

sentence **sentences**
A **sentence** is a group of words that tell you something. When you write a **sentence** down, you begin with a capital letter and end with a full stop.

separate **separates, separating, separated**
1 Two things that are **separate** are not connected in any way.
2 You **separate** things when you make them come apart.

September
September is the ninth month of the year. It has 30 days.

sequence **sequences**
A **sequence** is a group of things that come in a certain order.
*What is the next number in the **sequence** 5, 10, 15?*

serve **serves, serving, served**
1 If you **serve** food or drink to someone, you give it to them.
2 Someone who **serves** in a shop helps people to buy what they want.

set **sets, setting, set**
1 A **set** is a group of things that belong together.
*Shall we get out the chess **set**?*
2 When something **sets**, it goes hard or firm.
*We'll turn out the jelly when it's **set**.*

several
Several means more than two but not many.

sew **sews, sewing, sewed, sewn**
If you **sew**, you use a needle and thread to join two things together.
*Mum is **sewing** a button onto my coat.*

sex **sexes**
People and animals are divided into two groups, males and females.
These groups are called the **sexes**.

a
b
c
d
e
f
g
h
i
j
k
l
m
n
o
p
q
r
Ss
t
u
v
w
x
y
z

a
b
c
d
e
f
g
h
i
j
k
l
m
n
o
p
q
r

Ss

t
u
v
w
x
y
z

shade

If you are in the **shade**, you are in a place that the sunlight does not reach.

*It's too hot. Let's sit in the **shade** of that umbrella.*

shadow   shadows

If you stand in front of the light, you make a dark shape called a **shadow**.

shake   shakes, shaking, shook, shaken

If you **shake** something, you move it quickly from side to side.

shallow   shallower, shallowest

Something **shallow** is not very deep.

*Amy sat in a **shallow** pool.*

shampoo   shampoos

Shampoo is the soapy liquid you use for washing your hair.

shape   shapes

The **shape** of something is the pattern made by its outside edges. You use words like *square, oval* and *cone* to describe the **shapes** of things.

*You can see lots of **shapes** on page 184.*

share   shares, sharing, shared

1 When something is divided between two or more people, it is **shared**.

2 Each person gets a **share** of something that is divided up between them.

shark   sharks

A **shark** is a large, powerful fish with a lot of sharp teeth. **Sharks** live in the sea.

sharp   sharper, sharpest

1 Something **sharp** can cut or prick things easily.

*A knife has a **sharp** edge.*

*A pin has a **sharp** point.*

2 A **sharp** change is very sudden.

*There was a **sharp** bend in the road.*

shave   shaves, shaving, shaved

When someone **shaves**, they cut the hair from their skin to make it smooth.

shed   sheds, shedding, shed

1 A **shed** is a small building. People store garden tools in a **shed**.

2 If you **shed** something, you take it off or let it fall off.

*Trees **shed** their leaves in the autumn.*

sheep   sheep

A **sheep** is a farm animal that eats grass. **Sheep** are kept for wool and meat.

sheet **sheets**
 1 A **sheet** is a large piece of thin cloth that you put on a bed.
 2 A **sheet** of paper or glass is a piece of it.

shelf **shelves**
 A **shelf** is a long, flat piece of wood fixed to a wall. You keep things like books on **shelves**.

shell **shells**
 A **shell** is the hard outer part of a nut, egg or seed. Animals like snails, crabs and tortoises have **shells**, too.
 *The **shells** you pick up on the beach used to be the **shells** of little creatures.*

shelter **shelters, sheltering, sheltered**
 1 A **shelter** is a place that protects you.
 *I stood in the bus **shelter** to keep dry.*
 2 If you **shelter** from the rain, you stay somewhere dry.

shelves See **shelf**.

shepherd **shepherds**
 A **shepherd** looks after sheep.

shin **shins**
 Your **shin** is the front of your leg below the knee. (See page 174.)

shine **shines, shining, shone or shined**
 1 When something **shines,** it gives out bright light.
 2 When you **shine** an object, you rub it to make it bright.

shiny **shinier, shiniest**
 Shiny things are bright.

ship **ships**
 A **ship** is a large boat. **Ships** carry people and things across the sea.

shirt **shirts**
 A **shirt** is a piece of clothing that you wear on the top part of your body. It often has a collar and buttons.

shiver **shivers, shivering, shivered**
 When you **shiver**, your body shakes, usually because you are cold.

shoe **shoes**
 You wear **shoes** on your feet. They are usually made of leather or plastic and have a hard bottom surface.

shoelace **shoelaces**
 A **shoelace** is used to fasten some shoes. It goes through holes in the front of the shoe and is tied in a bow.

a
b
c
d
e
f
g
h
i
j
k
l
m
n
o
p
q
r
Ss
t
u
v
w
x
y
z

a
b
c
d
e
f
g
h
i
j
k
l
m
n
o
p
q
r

Ss

t
u
v
w
x
y
z

shone See **shine**.

shook See **shake**.

shoot **shoots, shooting, shot**
1 If someone **shoots**, they make something go very fast out of a gun or a bow.
2 A **shoot** is the part of a plant that you see when it first comes up through the ground.

shop **shops, shopping, shopped**
1 A **shop** is a place where things are sold.
2 When you **shop**, you go to the **shops** to buy things.

shore **shores**
The **shore** is the flat land at the edge of a sea or lake.

short **shorter, shortest**
1 A **short** person is not very tall.
2 Something **short** is not very long.
*My story is very **short**, so it will only take a few minutes to read.*

shorts
Shorts are short trousers that end above the knees. (See page 177.)

shot See **shoot**.

shoulder **shoulders**
Your **shoulder** is where your arm joins your body. (See page 174.)

shout **shouts, shouting, shouted**
1 If you **shout**, you call out loudly.
2 A **shout** is a loud call or cry.

show **shows, showing, showed, shown**
1 If you **show** something to someone, you let them see it.
2 If you **show** someone how to do something, you let them watch you doing it.
3 If you see a **show**, you watch something for fun.

shower **showers**
1 If you have a **shower**, you stand under a spray of water in the bathroom and wash yourself.
2 A **shower** is rain or snow that only falls for a short time.

shown See **show**.

shrink **shrinks, shrinking, shrank, shrunk**
If something **shrinks**, it becomes smaller.

shut   shuts, shutting, shut
If you **shut** something, you move part of it so that it is no longer open.
Shut the door to keep out the cold.

shy   shyer, shyest
A **shy** person is nervous about meeting people.
My baby sister is so shy that she cries if someone new talks to her!

sick
Someone who is **sick** is ill.
Our teacher has been away for a week because he is sick.

side   sides
1 A **side** is the left or right part of something.

2 The **sides** of an object can also be its flat faces.

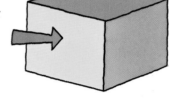

3 A **side** of a flat shape is the straight line between two corners.

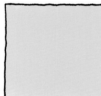

4 A team of players in a match can be called a **side**.

sideways
If you move **sideways**, you go to your left or right but keep facing forwards.

sigh   sighs, sighing, sighed
When you **sigh**, you breathe out slowly and make a sad sound. People **sigh** when they are sad, bored or tired.

sign   signs
A **sign** is a notice that gives you information using words or pictures.

signal   signals
1 A **signal** is a sound or action that tells people something.
When I blow my whistle, that's the signal for the end of playtime.
2 A railway **signal** tells train drivers whether they can go or must stop.

silent
If you are **silent**, you make no noise.

silk
Silk is a smooth, shiny cloth. It is made from threads spun by a silkworm.

silly   sillier, silliest
A **silly** person is not being sensible.
It was silly of you to go out in the rain without a coat!

silver
Silver is a shiny, grey metal. It is often used to make rings and earrings.

sing   sings, singing, sang, sung
When you **sing**, you make musical sounds with your voice.
Harry is singing his favourite song.

a
b
c
d
e
f
g
h
i
j
k
l
m
n
o
p
q
r

Ss

t
u
v
w
x
y
z

single
Single means only one and not more.
*We won the match by a **single** point.*

singular
You use the **singular** form of a word when you are talking about one person or thing.
*The **singular** of "children" is "child".*

sink sinks, sinking, sank, sunk
1 If something **sinks**, it moves downwards through water.
2 You can wash up in the kitchen **sink**.

sip sips, sipping, sipped
If you **sip** a drink, you take it a little at a time.

sister sisters
Your **sister** is a girl who has the same parents as you.

sit sits, sitting, sat
When you **sit**, you rest your bottom on something.

size sizes
The **size** of something is how big it is.
*The popcorn comes in three **sizes** – small, medium and large. Which **size** do you want?*

Small Medium Large

skate skates
A **skate** is a special boot. An ice **skate** has a blade fixed under it and a roller **skate** has wheels.
*The blade on one of my ice **skates** is broken.*

skateboard skateboards
A **skateboard** is a board on wheels. You stand on it with both feet.

skeleton skeletons
Your **skeleton** is all your bones joined up. It holds up your body.

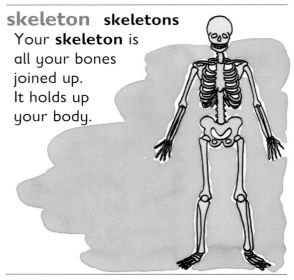

skill skills
If you have a **skill**, you can do something well.
*Reading and writing are very useful **skills**.*

skin
Your **skin** covers the outside of your body. Animals have many different kinds of **skin**. Some fruit and vegetables have **skin**, too.
*I peeled the banana and threw away the **skin**.*

skip skips, skipping, skipped
When you **skip**, you move forwards with little jumps from one foot to the other. Sometimes you **skip** with a rope.

skirt skirts
A **skirt** is a piece of clothing worn by girls and women. It hangs down from the waist. (See page 176.)

skull skulls
Your **skull** is the bony part of your head. Your brain is inside your **skull**.

sky skies
The **sky** is the space above the Earth where you see the sun, clouds and stars.

sledge sledges
You use a **sledge** to slide over snow. A large **sledge** is sometimes pulled by dogs.

sleep sleeps, sleeping, slept
When you **sleep**, your eyes are closed and you do not know what is happening around you.

sleeve sleeves
A **sleeve** is the part of a jacket, shirt or blouse that covers your arm.

slept See **sleep**.

slice slices
A **slice** is a thin piece cut from something bigger.
*May I have another **slice** of bread, please?*

slide slides, sliding, slid
1 When something **slides**, it moves quickly over a smooth surface.
2 A **slide** is an outdoor toy. You climb to the top and **slide** down.

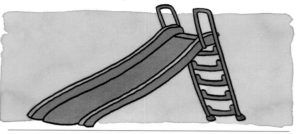

slip slips, slipping, slipped
If you **slip**, you fall down because you slide by accident.

slipper slippers
Slippers are soft shoes that you wear indoors.

slippery
If something is **slippery**, it is difficult to hold or walk on because it is wet or very smooth.
On an icy day, the playground is very slippery.

slope slopes
A **slope** is a piece of ground or a surface that is higher at one end than the other.

slow slower, slowest
If something is **slow**, it takes a long time.

slowly
If you do something **slowly**, you take a long time to do it.

a b c d e f g h i j k l m n o p q r **Ss** t u v w x y z

a
b
c
d
e
f
g
h
i
j
k
l
m
n
o
p
q
r
Ss
t
u
v
w
x
y
z

slug slugs

A **slug** is a small animal that moves slowly. It is like a snail without its shell.

small smaller, smallest

A **small** person or thing is not very big.

A mouse is a small animal.

smart smarter, smartest

1 If you look **smart**, you look neat and tidy.
2 **Smart** also means clever.

smash smashes, smashing, smashed

If something **smashes**, it breaks into lots of pieces.

Dad dropped the cup and it smashed on the floor.

smell smells, smelling, smelled or smelt

1 When you **smell** something, you notice it with your nose.

I could smell something burning.

2 You notice a **smell** by using your nose.

There was a smell of burning.

smile smiles, smiling, smiled

1 When you **smile**, your face looks happy.
2 A **smile** is a look of happiness on your face.

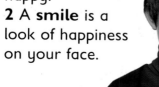

smoke

Smoke is the white or grey cloud that goes into the air when something burns.

When Dad lit the bonfire, smoke filled the air.

smooth smoother, smoothest

If something is **smooth**, it has no lumps or rough bits.

Toads have bumps, but frogs are smooth.

snack snacks

A **snack** is a small, quick meal.

We had a couple of sandwiches as a snack.

snail snails

A **snail** is a small, soft creature with a shell on its back. It moves very slowly.

snake snakes

A **snake** is a long, thin reptile with scales and no legs. Some **snakes** are dangerous to humans.

snap snaps, snapping, snapped

If something **snaps**, it breaks suddenly with a sharp noise.

A twig snapped under my foot.

sneeze **sneezes, sneezing, sneezed**
When you **sneeze**, you suddenly push air out through your nose, making a loud noise.
I had a bad cold and couldn't stop sneezing.

snow **snows, snowing, snowed**
1 Snow is soft, white frozen water that falls from the sky when it is cold.
2 It **snows** when **snow** falls from the sky.

snowball **snowballs**
A **snowball** is a small ball of snow. People make **snowballs** and throw them at each other for fun.

snowflake **snowflakes**
A **snowflake** is a single piece of snow as it falls.

snowman **snowmen**
A **snowman** is snow made into the shape of a person.

soak **soaks, soaking, soaked**
If you **soak** something, you leave it in liquid.
Mum soaked my dirty socks in water overnight.

soap **soaps**
You use **soap** and water to wash yourself or your clothes.

sock **socks**
You wear **socks** on your feet to keep them warm. (See page 177.)

sofa **sofas**
A **sofa** is a long, soft seat with arms and a back. Two or three people can sit on a **sofa**.

soft **softer, softest**
If something is **soft**, it sinks down when you press it.
My head sank into the soft pillow.

soil
Soil is the top layer of earth that plants grow in.

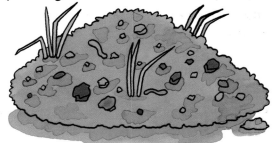

sold See **sell**.

soldier **soldiers**
A **soldier** belongs to an army.

solid
1 A **solid** material feels firm and does not change shape easily.
Wood is solid but oil and water are liquid.
2 Something **solid** is not hollow.

solve **solves, solving, solved**
If you **solve** a problem, you find the answer to it.

a
b
c
d
e
f
g
h
i
j
k
l
m
n
o
p
q
r
Ss
t
u
v
w
x
y
z

a
b
c
d
e
f
g
h
i
j
k
l
m
n
o
p
q
r

Ss

t
u
v
w
x
y
z

some

You say **some** when you mean a number or amount but do not say it exactly.

*Please pass me **some** sausages and **some** mashed potato.*

somebody

Somebody is a person you do not name.

***Somebody** has left their coat behind.*

someone

Someone is another word for somebody.

something

Something is a thing that you do not describe.

*I can hear **something** banging.*

sometimes

Sometimes means quite often but not always.

*I'm **sometimes** allowed to stay up late on holiday.*

somewhere

If you say you went **somewhere**, you do not say exactly where.

son   sons

A person's **son** is their male child.

*Mr Jones has two **sons**.*

song   songs

When you sing a **song**, you sing words to a piece of music.

soon   sooner, soonest

Soon means not too long into the future.

*Today is Friday. **Soon** it will be the weekend.*

sore

If part of your body is **sore**, it hurts.

*I have a **sore** throat – it hurts when I swallow.*

sorry

You say that you are **sorry** when you have done something wrong.

*I'm **sorry** I'm late.*

sort   sorts, sorting, sorted

1 If things are the same **sort**, they are the same kind.

*Do you like this **sort** of chocolate?*

2 If you **sort** things, you put them into groups.

***Sort** these buttons into two piles – red ones and blue ones.*

sought   See seek.

sound   sounds

A **sound** is something you can hear.

*Can you hear the **sound** of the drums?*

soup   soups

Soup is a hot liquid food made from meat or vegetables.

sour

If something is **sour**, it has a sharp taste like a lemon.

*This milk tastes **sour**. Throw it away.*

south

South is a direction. It is on your right when you look towards the rising sun.

space spaces

1 A **space** is a gap or an empty place.

*Is there a **space** for me at your table?*

2 Space is all around the Earth where the planets and the stars are.

spaceship spaceships

A **spaceship** is a vehicle that can travel through space.

spade spades

A **spade** is a tool used for digging. It has a long handle and a wide blade.

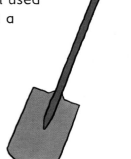

sparrow sparrows

A **sparrow** is a small brown bird found in many parts of the world.

speak speaks, speaking, spoke, spoken

When you **speak**, you say words out loud.

special

If something is **special**, it is better than other things of the same kind.

*Mum made a **special** meal for my birthday.*

speech

Speech is what you hear when someone is speaking.

speech marks

Speech marks are marks you use in writing to show when someone starts and stops speaking.

"I'm going out now," said Dad.

"Can I come?" I asked.

speech marks

speed speeds

The **speed** of something is how fast it is moving.

*The racing car was travelling at a very high **speed**.*

spell spells, spelling, spelled or spelt

1 When you **spell** a word, you say or write the letters in the right order.

*Please **spell** your name.*

2 In fairy stories, if someone says a **spell**, magic things happen.

a b c d e f g h i j k l m n o p q r **Ss** t u v w x y z

a b c d e f g h i j k l m n o p q r

Ss

t u v w x y z

spend spends, spending, spent
1 You **spend** money when you buy something with it.
2 You **spend** time when you use it.
*I **spent** three hours painting.*

sphere spheres
A **sphere** is an object that is round when you look at it from any direction. Footballs and planets are **spheres**.

spider spiders
A **spider** is a small animal with eight legs. It spins a web to catch insects for food.

spill spills, spilling, spilled or spilt
If you **spill** something, it runs out of a container by mistake.
*I **spilt** my drink all over my shirt!*

spin spins, spinning, spun
If something **spins**, it turns round very quickly.
*The washing machine **spins** our clothes.*

spine spines
1 Your **spine** is the long row of bones down the middle of your back.
2 A **spine** is a long, sharp point on an animal's body or a plant.

spiteful
A **spiteful** person says nasty things to people.

splash splashes
When something hits the water, it makes a **splash**.

split splits, splitting, split
If something **splits**, it divides into parts.

spoil spoils, spoiling, spoiled, spoilt
If something is **spoilt**, it is not as good as it was before.

spoke See **speak**.

spoon spoons
You use a **spoon** to eat soup and cereal, and to stir liquids.

sport sports
A **sport** is something that you do to keep fit and to have fun. Swimming, rounders and football are all **sports**.

spot spots
1 A **spot** is a round mark.
*A ladybird is red with black **spots**.*
2 A **spot** is also a small red mark on your skin.

spout spouts
You pour the water out of a jug or kettle through its **spout**.

spray **sprays, spraying, sprayed**
If you **spray** something, you make it wet with tiny drops of liquid.

spring **springs**
1 Spring is the season between winter and summer. The weather gets warmer and plants start to grow again.
2 A **spring** is a curly piece of metal. It jumps back to its normal shape after you press it down.

spun See **spin**.

square **squares**
1 A **square** is a shape with four equal sides and four corners that are all right angles.
2 Anything that has this shape is **square**.

squash **squashes, squashing, squashed**
1 Squash is a drink made from fruit, sugar and water.
2 If you **squash** something, you press it so that it goes flat.
*Emily sat on her hat and **squashed** it flat.*

squeak **squeaks, squeaking, squeaked**
If something **squeaks**, it makes a short, high noise.
*My new shoes **squeak** when I walk.*

squeeze **squeezes, squeezing, squeezed**
If you **squeeze** something, you press its sides together.
*Mum **squeezed** the oranges to get the juice out.*

squirrel **squirrels**
A **squirrel** is a small animal with a long, thick tail. **Squirrels** live in trees and eat nuts.

stable **stables**
A horse is kept in a **stable**.

stage **stages**
A **stage** is a raised platform in a theatre or hall.
*At the pantomime, there was a horse on the **stage**.*

stair **stairs**
Stairs are a set of steps inside a building. You climb the **stairs** from one floor to the next.

stamp **stamps**
A **stamp** is a small piece of paper with a picture on it. You stick a **stamp** on a letter or parcel before you post it.

stand **stands, standing, stood**
When you **stand**, your feet stay in one place on the floor.

a b c d e f g h i j k l m n o p q r **Ss** t u v w x y z

143

a
b
c
d
e
f
g
h
i
j
k
l
m
n
o
p
q
r
Ss
t
u
v
w
x
y
z

star stars
1 A **star** is a tiny light in the sky at night.
2 A **star** is also a famous actor or performer.
3 A **star** can also be a shape with five or more points. (See page 184.)

stare stares, staring, stared
1 If you **stare** at something, you look at it for a long time.
2 A **stare** is a long look at something.

start starts, starting, started
If you **start** to do something, you begin to do it.
*I've just **started** my homework.*

station stations
1 Trains and buses stop for passengers at a **station**.
2 A **station** is also a building with a special use, like a police **station**.
*We went to the petrol **station** for some petrol.*

statue statues
A **statue** is a figure of a person or animal. **Statues** are made from stone or metal.

stay stays, staying, stayed
1 If you **stay** in a place, you do not move away from it.
2 If you **stay** in a hotel, you sleep there.

steady steadier, steadiest
If something is **steady**, it does not shake or move.
*Please hold the ladder **steady**.*

steal steals, stealing, stole, stolen
If you **steal** something, you take something that belongs to someone else.

steam
Steam is the white cloud you see above very hot water. It is made of tiny drops of water.
***Steam** was coming off the hot tea.*

steel
Steel is a strong metal.

steep steeper, steepest
A **steep** slope goes up sharply.
*We pushed our bikes up the hill because it was too **steep** to ride them.*

stem stems
The **stem** of a plant holds the leaves and flowers away from the soil.

step steps, stepping, stepped
1 You **step** when you move your foot up and down when you walk.
2 A **step** is also where you put your foot on the stairs or a ladder.
*There are 12 **steps** up to Gran's flat.*

stereo **stereos**
A **stereo** is a machine for playing tapes and CDs.

stick **sticks, sticking, stuck**
1 A **stick** is a long, thin piece of wood.
2 If you **stick** one thing to another, you fix it with glue or tape.
3 If you **stick** a pointed object into something, you push it in so that it stays there.

stiff **stiffer, stiffest**
If something is **stiff**, it is hard to bend.
*The boxes were made of **stiff** cardboard.*

still
1 If something is **still** happening, it has not stopped yet.
*It's been raining all day and it's **still** raining.*
2 If you are **still**, you are not moving.
*Stand **still** while I button your coat.*

sting **stings, stinging, stung**
If something **stings** you, it pricks your skin and hurts you.
*A bee **stung** Anya in the arm.*

stir **stirs, stirring, stirred**
When you **stir** a liquid, you use a spoon or a stick to move it around.

stole See **steal**.

stolen See **steal**.

stomach **stomachs**
When you swallow your food, it goes into your **stomach**.

stone **stones**
1 **Stone** is a hard, dry material. It is used for building houses and walls. You find small **stones** on the ground.
2 The hard seed in the middle of a peach or a plum is called a **stone**.

stood See **stand**.

stop **stops, stopping, stopped**
1 If you **stop** doing something, you do not do it any more.
2 If someone **stops** you doing something, they do not let you do it.
3 A bus lets people on or off at a bus **stop**.

store **stores, storing, stored**
1 If you **store** something, you keep it until it is needed.
2 A **store** is a large shop which sells lots of different things.

storm **storms**
In a **storm** it rains hard and strong winds blow. There is often thunder and lightning.

a
b
c
d
e
f
g
h
i
j
k
l
m
n
o
p
q
r
Ss
t
u
v
w
x
y
z

a
b
c
d
e
f
g
h
i
j
k
l
m
n
o
p
q
r

Ss

t
u
v
w
x
y
z

story   **stories**
A **story** tells you about people and what happened to them. Some **stories** are made up, others are about real people.

straight   **straighter, straightest**
Something **straight** is not bent or curved.
*Lisa has **straight** hair.*

strange   **stranger, strangest**
Something **strange** seems odd and unusual.
*The alien had **strange** yellow eyes.*

straw   **straws**
1 Farm animals sleep on **straw**. It is the dry stems from wheat and corn.
2 A **straw** is a thin plastic tube that you can drink through.

strawberry   **strawberries**
A **strawberry** is a small, soft, red fruit. It has tiny seeds on its surface.

stream   **streams**
A **stream** is a small river.

street   **streets**
A **street** is a road in a town. It has shops and houses along it.

strength
Your **strength** is your energy and power.
*I haven't got the **strength** to lift that suitcase.*

stretch   **stretches, stretching, stretched**
When you **stretch** something, you pull it to make it longer or wider.
*David **stretched** the rubber band.*

strict   **stricter, strictest**
A **strict** person makes people behave well and do what they should.

string   **strings**
1 String is thin rope used for tying things together.
2 You play on the **strings** of violins and guitars to make music.

strip   **strips**
A **strip** is a long, thin piece of something.

stripe   **stripes**
A **stripe** is a line on something.
*Zebras have **stripes** on their bodies.*

strong   **stronger, strongest**
1 A **strong** person can lift heavy things.
2 You cannot easily break something that is **strong**.

stuck   See **stick**.

stung   See **sting**.

submarine **submarines**

A **submarine** is a ship that can travel under water.

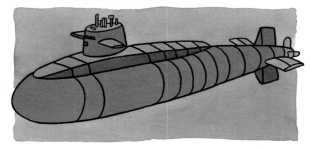

subtract **subtracts, subtracting, subtracted**

If you **subtract** one number from another, you take it away and count what is left. The symbol − means **subtract**, or minus.

*Three **subtract** two leaves one.* 3 − 2 = 1

subtraction

Subtraction is what you do when you take one number from another and count what is left.

succeed **succeeds, succeeding, succeeded**

If you **succeed**, you do what you have tried to do.

*Becky **succeeded** in getting into the team.*

suck **sucks, sucking, sucked**

If you **suck** something, you pull at it with your mouth.

sudden

If something is **sudden**, it happens without warning.

*The dog gave a **sudden** bark.*

suddenly

If something happens **suddenly**, you are not expecting it to happen.

*The lights **suddenly** went out.*

sugar

Sugar is used to make food and drink sweet.

suit **suits**

A **suit** is trousers or a skirt worn with a jacket of the same material.

suitcase **suitcases**

When you go on holiday, you carry your clothes in a **suitcase**.

sum **sums**

The **sum** of two or more numbers is what they make when you add them together.

13+5=18

summer

Summer is the season between spring and autumn. The weather is warm and the days are long.

sun

The **sun** is a star. It shines in the sky during the day and gives us heat and light. The Earth travels around the **sun** once a year.

a b c d e f g h i j k l m n o p q r **Ss** t u v w x y z

a
b
c
d
e
f
g
h
i
j
k
l
m
n
o
p
q
r

Ss

t
u
v
w
x
y
z

Sunday **Sundays**
Sunday is the day of the week between Saturday and Monday.

sung See **sing**.

sunk See **sink**.

sunny **sunnier, sunniest**
When the weather is **sunny**, the sun is shining brightly.

sunshine
The light that comes from the sun is called **sunshine**.

supermarket **supermarkets**
A **supermarket** is a very large shop that sells food and other things. You take what you want as you go around and pay for it on the way out.

supper **suppers**
Supper is a light meal eaten in the evening.

sure
If you are **sure** that something is true, you believe it is true.

surface **surfaces**
The **surface** of something is the top or outside of it.
*The **surface** of the table was very shiny.*

surprise **surprises, surprising, surprised**
1 A **surprise** is something that you did not expect.
2 You **surprise** someone when you do something they were not expecting.
*We **surprised** my mum by taking her breakfast in bed.*

swallow **swallows, swallowing, swallowed**
1 When you **swallow** something, it goes down your throat and into your stomach.
2 A **swallow** is also a bird. It has a forked tail.

swam See **swim**.

swan **swans**
A **swan** is a very large white bird with a long curved neck. **Swans** live on rivers or lakes.

sweep **sweeps, sweeping, swept**
You **sweep** a floor with a brush to make it clean.

sweet **sweeter, sweetest; sweets**
1 **Sweet** food tastes of sugar.
2 A **sweet** person is friendly and loving.
3 Toffees and chocolates are **sweets**.
4 A **sweet** is also a pudding.

swept See **sweep**.

swim **swims, swimming, swam, swum**
You **swim** by using your arms and legs to move through the water.

swimming pool **swimming pools**
A **swimming pool** is a large hole in the ground that is filled with water for swimming.

swing **swings, swinging, swung**
1 A **swing** is a seat hung on chains or ropes. It moves backwards and forwards when you push it.
2 When something **swings**, it moves backwards and forwards in the air.

switch **switches**
You press on a **switch** to start a machine or turn on a light.

sword **swords**
A **sword** is a long metal blade with a handle. People fought with **swords** many years ago.

swum See **swim**.

swung See **swing**.

syllable **syllables**
A **syllable** is a word or part of a word that has one separate sound when you say it.
"Girl" has one ***syllable*** *and "sister" has two* ***syllables***.

symbol **symbols**
A **symbol** is a letter, number or other mark that is used to mean something else.
+ is a ***symbol*** *that means add.*

symmetrical
If something is **symmetrical**, you can divide it into two equal and matching halves.

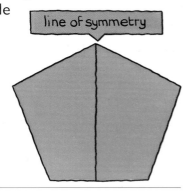
line of symmetry

symmetry
A line of **symmetry** can be drawn between the two halves of something that is symmetrical.

synonym **synonyms**
A **synonym** is a word that means the same or almost the same as another word.
(See page 180.)

syrup
Syrup is a sweet, thick liquid made by boiling sugar with water.

a
b
c
d
e
f
g
h
i
j
k
l
m
n
o
p
q
r
Ss
t
u
v
w
x
y
z

table tables

1 A **table** is a flat surface with legs. You can work or eat at a **table**.

2 A **table** is also a way of showing information.

Day	Weather
Monday	Sunny
Tuesday	Rainy and cool
Wednesday	Showers

tadpole tadpoles

A **tadpole** is a tiny black animal that lives in water. It grows into a frog.

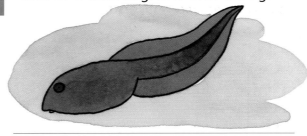

tail tails

An animal's **tail** grows at the back end of its body.

*A dog wags its **tail** when it is happy.*

take takes, taking, took, taken

1 When you **take** something, you move it from a place.

2 If you **take** one number away from another, you subtract it and count what is left. **Take away** means the same as subtract.

tale tales

A **tale** is an old word for a story.

talk talks, talking, talked

When you **talk**, you say words out loud.

tall taller, tallest

The top of a **tall** person or object is a long way from the ground.

tally tallies

If you keep a **tally**, you record the number of times something happens.

tame tamer, tamest

A **tame** animal is friendly towards humans.

*Charlotte's **tame** lamb follows her everywhere.*

tank tanks

1 A **tank** is a large container for liquids like petrol or water.

2 A **tank** is also a large fighting vehicle. It has a gun on top.

tap taps, tapping, tapped
1 You turn on a **tap** to run water into a sink or a bath.
2 If you **tap** something, you hit it gently.
*Mike **tapped** me on the shoulder and said hello.*

tape tapes
1 Tape is material in a long strip. You can use it to fasten something.
2 You can record sound or pictures onto **tape**.
*We need a new **tape** for the video recorder.*

tape measure tape measures
A **tape measure** is a strip of cloth or soft plastic marked into units. It is used for measuring.

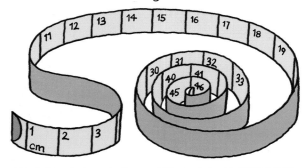

tart tarts
A **tart** is a round pastry case with a filling. It is often filled with fruit.

taste tastes, tasting, tasted
If you **taste** something, you put it in your mouth to find out what it is like to eat.

taught See **teach**.

taxi taxis
A **taxi** is a car that you pay to travel in.

tea
Tea is a hot drink. You make it by pouring boiling water onto dried leaves or a tea bag.

teach teaches, teaching, taught
If you **teach** someone, you show them how to do something.
*Can you **teach** me how to ride a bike?*

teacher teachers
A **teacher** helps people to learn something or shows them how to do something.

team teams
A **team** is a group of people who play or work together.

tear tears, tearing, tore, torn
1 (*sounds like* **hair**) If you **tear** something, you pull it apart.
2 (*sounds like* **here**) A **tear** is a drop of liquid that falls from your eye when you cry.

teaspoon teaspoons
A **teaspoon** is a small spoon used for stirring drinks.
*Add two **teaspoons** of sugar.*

teddy teddies
A **teddy**, or **teddy bear**, is a soft toy bear.

a b c d e f g h i j k l m n o p q r s **Tt** u v w x y z

a b c d e f g h i j k l m n o p q r s **Tt** u v w x y z

teeth See **tooth**.

telephone **telephones**
You use a **telephone** to speak to someone in another place.

television **televisions**
A **television** turns waves in the air into pictures and sounds. It is often called a TV.

tell **tells, telling, told**
If you **tell** someone about something, you share what you know with them.

temple **temples**
A **temple** is a place where people go to pray.

tent **tents**
You can sleep outdoors in a **tent**. It is made from a piece of cloth stretched over metal poles.

term **terms**
A school **term** is the time when you go to school between two holidays.

terrible
Something **terrible** is very frightening or nasty.
*There was a **terrible** storm last night.*

test **tests**
When you do a **test**, you answer questions to show what you can do.

text **texts**
The words in a book or poem are its **text**.

thank **thanks, thanking, thanked**
You **thank** someone who has given you something or has done something for you.
Thank you for my new shirt, Gran!

theatre **theatres**
You go to a **theatre** to see a show, a play or a pantomime.

theme **themes**
A **theme** of a story is the important thought that runs through it.

then
1 If something happened **then**, it happened at that time.
*We were living in our old house **then**.*
2 Then also tells you what happened next.
*First we watched a really good video, **then** we had dinner.*

thick **thicker, thickest**
1 If something is **thick**, it is a large distance from one side to the other.
*Jason likes **thick** bread but Katy prefers thin slices.*

2 A **thick** liquid flows slowly.

thief **thieves**
A **thief** is someone who steals things.

thigh **thighs**
Your **thigh** is the part of your leg between your knee and your hip. (See page 174.)

thin **thinner, thinnest**
1 Something is **thin** if there is only a short distance from one side to the other.
2 A **thin** person is not fat.

thing **things**
A **thing** is something that is not alive.

think **thinks, thinking, thought**
When you **think**, you use your brain to work something out.

thirsty **thirstier, thirstiest**
If you are **thirsty**, you need a drink.

thought See **think**.

thousand **thousands**
A **thousand** is the number 1000. It is ten hundreds.

thread **threads**
A **thread** is a fine string. You use it to sew things together.

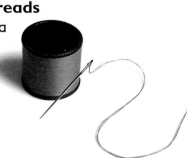

threw See **throw**.

throat **throats**
Your **throat** is the front part of your neck.

through
If you go **through** something, you go from one side of it to the other.

throw **throws, throwing, threw, thrown**
When you **throw** something, you use your hand to make it travel through the air.

thumb **thumbs**
Your **thumb** is the short finger on the inside of your hand. (See page 174.)

thunder
Thunder is the sound that follows lightning during a storm.

thunderstorm **thunderstorms**
In a **thunderstorm**, there is thunder and lightning.

a
b
c
d
e
f
g
h
i
j
k
l
m
n
o
p
q
r
s
Tt
u
v
w
x
y
z

Thursday **Thursdays**
Thursday is the day of the week between Wednesday and Friday.

tick **ticks**
1 A **tick** is a mark written ✔. It shows that an answer is correct.
2 The **tick** of a clock is the sound it makes every second.

ticket **tickets**
You buy a **ticket** to travel on a bus, train or plane. You also often need a **ticket** to go to something.
*I've got two **tickets** for the concert.*

tidy **tidier, tidiest**
If a room is **tidy**, everything is neat and in the right place.

tie **ties, tying, tied**
1 You **tie** things together by making a knot or a bow.

2 People wear a **tie** around the neck of a shirt. (See page 177.)

tiger **tigers**
A **tiger** is a fierce wild cat with orange fur and black stripes. **Tigers** live in Asia.

tight **tighter, tightest**
If something is **tight**, it fits closely.
*These trousers are too **tight**.*

tights
Tights cover your legs from your waist down to your feet. They are worn mainly by girls and women.

till
Till means until.
*I'll stay **till** your dad comes home.*

time
Seconds, minutes, hours, days, weeks, months and years are all measures of **time**. (See page 178.)

timer **timers**
A **timer** is a kind of clock. It can be set to measure the time left until something happens.
*I've set the **timer** to ring after ten minutes.*

times
Times is another way of saying multiplied by. The symbol × means **times**.
*Three **times** two equals six. $3 \times 2 = 6$*

tin **tins**
A **tin** is a small metal container. Food and paint come in **tins**.
*Our dog eats a **tin** of dog food every day.*

tiny **tinier, tiniest**
Something **tiny** is very small.

tip tips
1 A **tip** is a piece of helpful information.
2 The **tip** of something is the very end of it.
*Can you touch your nose with the **tip** of your tongue?*

tired
If you are **tired**, you need to go to sleep.

title titles
The **title** of a book or poem is what the writer has called it.
*The **title** of this book is Collins First School Dictionary.*

toad toads
A **toad** is an animal like a large frog.

toast
Toast is a slice of bread that is cooked until it is light brown. It is often eaten with butter.

today
Today is the day you are in now.
*It is my birthday **today**.*

toe toes
You have five **toes** on the end of each foot. (See page 174.)

toffee toffees
Toffee is a chewy sweet.

toilet toilets
You go to the **toilet** to empty waste from your body.

told See **tell**.

tomato tomatoes
A **tomato** is a red fruit. You often eat it raw.

tomorrow
Tomorrow is the day that comes after today.

tongue tongues
Your **tongue** is inside your mouth. You use it when you speak or eat.
*My sister likes to stick out her **tongue**.*

tongue twister
tongue twisters
A **tongue twister** is difficult to say quickly and correctly.
*"Red lorry, yellow lorry" is a well-known **tongue twister**.*

tonight
Tonight means the end of today.
*Will you come with me to the match **tonight**?*

took See **take**.

tool tools
You use a **tool** to make or fix things.
*My dad uses special **tools** when he repairs the car.*

a
b
c
d
e
f
g
h
i
j
k
l
m
n
o
p
q
r
s
Tt
u
v
w
x
y
z

a
b
c
d
e
f
g
h
i
j
k
l
m
n
o
p
q
r
s
Tt
u
v
w
x
y
z

tooth **teeth**
You have hard, white, bony **teeth** inside your mouth. You use them when you chew or bite.

toothbrush **toothbrushes**
You use a **toothbrush** to clean your teeth.

toothpaste
You spread **toothpaste** on a toothbrush when you clean your teeth.

top **tops**
The **top** of something is its highest part.
*They climbed to the very **top** of the mountain.*

torch **torches**
A **torch** is a light you can carry.

tore See **tear**.

torn See **tear**.

tortoise **tortoises**
A **tortoise** is a reptile with a shell on its back. It moves very slowly.

toss **tosses, tossing, tossed**
When you **toss** something, you throw it in the air.

total **totals**
When you add things up, you work out their **total**.

touch **touches, touching, touched**
1 When you **touch** something, you put your hand on it.
2 When things **touch**, they are placed against each other.

tough **tougher, toughest**
Tough means very strong and not easily broken.

tow **tows, towing, towed**
If you **tow** something, you pull it along behind you.
*The car **towed** a caravan.*

towel **towels**
You dry yourself with a **towel**.

tower **towers**
A **tower** is a tall building. It is often part of another building.

town **towns**
A **town** is a collection of homes and businesses. It is larger than a village and smaller than a city.

toy **toys**
A **toy** is something that you play with for fun.

trace **traces, tracing, traced**
When you **trace** something, you make a copy by drawing over it through a piece of clear paper.

track tracks

1 A **track** is a path for people or animals.

2 Railway trains run on **track** made from long strips of metal.

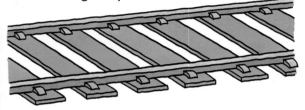

tractor tractors

A **tractor** is a vehicle that is used on a farm.

traffic

Traffic is all the vehicles on the roads at one time.

traffic light traffic lights

Traffic lights tell traffic when to go or stop. They are red, yellow and green.

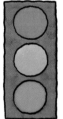

trail trails

A **trail** is a path or marks that you can follow.

train trains

A **train** is an engine and carriages that run on railway track.

trap traps, trapping, trapped

If you are **trapped**, you are in a place that you cannot get out of.

travel travels, travelling, travelled

When you **travel**, you go on a journey.

treasure treasures

A **treasure** is something valuable.

tree trees

A **tree** is a large plant. It has a wooden trunk and branches with leaves on.

triangle triangles

A **triangle** is a flat shape with three sides.

triangular

Anything in the shape of a triangle is **triangular**.

trick tricks, tricking, tricked

1 If you **trick** someone, you make them believe something that is not true.

2 A **trick** is also a piece of magic.

tried See **try**.

tries See **try**.

trim trims, trimming, trimmed

If you **trim** something, you cut it to make it neat and tidy.

*Dad is **trimming** the hedge.*

a
b
c
d
e
f
g
h
i
j
k
l
m
n
o
p
q
r
s
Tt
u
v
w
x
y
z

a
b
c
d
e
f
g
h
i
j
k
l
m
n
o
p
q
r
s
Tt
u
v
w
x
y
z

trip **trips, tripping, tripped**
1 If you **trip** over something, you catch your foot on it and fall over.
2 If you go on a **trip**, you travel somewhere.
*Lou is going on a **trip** to a museum.*

trolley **trolleys**
A **trolley** has wheels and a handle. You use it to move heavy things.

trouble
1 You get into **trouble** if you do something wrong.
*If I'm late home I'll get into **trouble**.*
2 If you have **trouble**, you have a problem.

trousers
You wear **trousers** to cover your body from your waist to your ankles. **Trousers** have separate legs.

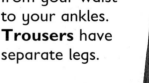

truck **trucks**
A **truck** is a short, heavy vehicle. It is used for carrying things.

true **truer, truest**
If something is **true**, it really happened.

trumpet **trumpets**
A **trumpet** is a musical instrument made of metal. You blow through it to make a sound.

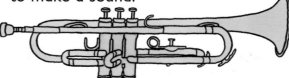

trunk **trunks**
1 The part of a tree that grows up from the ground is called a **trunk**.
2 An elephant's long nose is called a **trunk**.

trust **trusts, trusting, trusted**
If you **trust** someone, you believe they will do what they say.

truth
When you tell the **truth,** you say what really happened.

try **tries, trying, tried**
When you **try** to do something, you do it as well as you can.

T-shirt **T-shirts**
A **T-shirt** is a soft cotton shirt with short sleeves and no collar.

tube **tubes**
A **tube** is a hollow cylinder.

tuck **tucks, tucking, tucked**
1 If you **tuck** someone in, you make them comfortable in bed.
2 When you **tuck** into food, you start to eat it.

Tuesday **Tuesdays**
Tuesday is the day of the week between Monday and Wednesday.

tug-of-war

A **tug-of-war** is a contest. Two teams pull on the ends of a rope. The winners pull the other side over the winning line.

tumble tumbles, tumbling, tumbled

You **tumble** when you fall head over heels.

*Jack fell down and Jill came **tumbling** after him.*

tummy tummies

Tummy is another word for stomach. When you swallow your food, it goes into your **tummy**.

tune tunes

A **tune** is the notes that go together to make a piece of music.

*That song has a **tune** that is easy to remember.*

tunnel tunnels

A **tunnel** is a long hole through the ground.

turn turns, turning, turned

1 When you **turn**, you move to your left or your right.
2 If people take **turns**, they do something one after another.
3 If something **turns** into something else, it changes.

*Water **turns** into ice when it freezes.*

turnip turnips

A **turnip** is a round vegetable that is white or yellow inside.

tusk tusks

A **tusk** is a large horn on the head of an elephant or rhinoceros.

TV TVs

TV is short for television.

twice

Twice means two times.
*Knock **twice** and then wait.*
Twice 3 is 6.

twig twigs

A **twig** is a small branch of a tree or bush.

twin twins

When a mother has **twins**, she has two babies at the same time. **Twins** often look alike.

twist twists, twisting, twisted

When you **twist** something, you bend it into a round shape.

tying See **tie**.

type types, typing, typed

1 When you **type** something, you use a keyboard to print letters.
2 A **type** is one kind of a thing.
*What **type** of shoes do you like best?*

tyre tyres

A **tyre** is a piece of thick rubber that goes round a wheel.

a b c d e f g h i j k l m n o p q r s **Tt** u v w x y z

a b c d e f g h i j k l m n o p q r s t **Uu** v w x y z

ugly **uglier, ugliest**
Something **ugly** is not nice to look at.

umbrella **umbrellas**
You put up an **umbrella** to keep you dry when it rains.

uncle **uncles**
Your **uncle** is the brother of your mother or father. Your aunt's husband is also your **uncle**.

underground
Underground means under the ground.

understand **understands, understanding, understood**
If you **understand** something, you know what it means.

undress **undresses, undressing, undressed**
When you **undress**, you take your clothes off.

uniform **uniforms**
Some people wear a **uniform** to show what job they do or where they go to school.

unit **units**
The **units** of a number are the ones.
*The number 37 has three tens and seven **units**.*

universe
The **universe** is space and all the stars and planets.

until
Until a time means finishing then.

upset
If you are **upset**, you are sad and may feel like crying.

upside down
If something is **upside down**, its top is where its bottom should be.

upstairs
If you go **upstairs**, you go up to a higher level of a building.

urgent
Something **urgent** must be done at once.

use **uses, using, used**
Something is **used** to do a job.

useful
Something **useful** is used to do a job.

usual
Something **usual** happens most of the time.

usually
Usually means often but not always.

Vv

vacuum cleaner
vacuum cleaners
A **vacuum cleaner**
is a machine
that sucks
up dust.

valley **valleys**
A **valley** is a low area of land
between hills or mountains.

valuable
Something **valuable** is worth a lot of
money.
The thief stole a valuable clock.

van **vans**
A **van** is a vehicle for carrying things.

vanish **vanishes, vanishing, vanished**
If something **vanishes**, you suddenly
cannot see it any more.
*I had my pencil a minute ago but now it's
vanished!*

vase **vases**
You put flowers
in a **vase**.

vegetable **vegetables**
A **vegetable** is a plant that you
grow for food. Potatoes, carrots and
peas are all **vegetables**. Salad is
made with raw **vegetables**.
*For dinner today we had meat with roast
potatoes and two other vegetables.*

vehicle **vehicles**
Any machine that you can travel
around in or on is a **vehicle**. Cars,
buses, vans and bicycles are all
vehicles.

verb **verbs**
A **verb** is a word that says what is
happening or being done.

The birds sang
as Patrick walked to school.
verbs

verse **verses**
A **verse** is a group of lines of a poem
or a song, like this:
Here we go round the mulberry bush,
The mulberry bush, the mulberry bush,
Here we go round the mulberry bush,
On a cold and frosty morning.

a
b
c
d
e
f
g
h
i
j
k
l
m
n
o
p
q
r
s
t
u

Vv

w
x
y
z

vest **vests**
A **vest** is a piece of clothing. It is worn under a shirt.

vet **vets**
A **vet** looks after sick animals.
*When our puppy was ill, the **vet** gave her some pills to make her better.*

video **videos, videoing, videoed**
1 A **video** is a tape with TV programmes or films recorded on it. You play a **video** on a **video** recorder and watch it on a television.
2 If you **video** something, you record pictures and sounds on tape.
3 A **video** camera records moving pictures and sound.

village **villages**
A **village** is a group of streets and houses. It is smaller than a town.

violin **violins**
A **violin** is a musical instrument made of wood. You play it by holding it under your chin and pulling a stick called a bow across the strings.

visible
If something is **visible**, you can see it.
*I'm just **visible** behind my mum in this photo.*

visit **visits, visiting, visited**
When you **visit** someone, you go to see them at their home.

visitor **visitors**
A **visitor** is someone who comes to visit you.
*We've got **visitors** coming to stay this weekend.*

voice **voices**
Your **voice** is the sound you make when you speak.
*I caught a bad cold and lost my **voice**.*

volcano **volcanoes**
A **volcano** is a mountain that sometimes throws smoke and melted rocks into the sky.

vote **votes, voting, voted**
You **vote** for someone or something by saying which you choose.
*We **voted** to buy a hamster as a class pet.*

vowel **vowels**
The **vowels** are the letters a, e, i, o and u. The other letters are consonants.

Ww

wagon wagons
A **wagon** is used to carry heavy things. It is usually pulled by horses.

waist waists
Your **waist** is the middle part of your body. (See page 174.)

wait waits, waiting, waited
If you **wait** for something, you don't do something until it happens.
*I am **waiting** for Kyle to help me.*

wake wakes, waking, woke, woken
You **wake** up when you stop being asleep.

walk walks, walking, walked
You **walk** by putting one foot in front of the other. **Walking** is slower than running.

wall walls
A **wall** of a building or room is one of its sides.
*I'll hang your picture on the **wall**.*

wand wands
A magician or wizard uses a small stick called a **wand** when they do magic tricks.

want wants, wanting, wanted
If you **want** something, you would like to have it.
*Bethany **wants** a banana.*

war wars
When countries go to **war**, their armies fight each other.

wardrobe wardrobes
A **wardrobe** is a large cupboard for keeping clothes in.

warm warmer, warmest
Warm means quite hot but not very hot.
*This bread is still **warm** from the oven.*

warn warns, warning, warned
You **warn** someone by telling them about something bad that might happen.
*The weather man **warned** us of storms and rain.*

warning warnings
A **warning** tells you that there is something bad or dangerous.
*The notice said: "**Warning**: fog".*

wash washes, washing, washed
You **wash** yourself with water to make your skin clean.

washing machine washing machines
A **washing machine** is a machine that washes clothes.

a b c d e f g h i j k l m n o p q r s t u v **Ww** x y z

a
b
c
d
e
f
g
h
i
j
k
l
m
n
o
p
q
r
s
t
u
v

Ww

x
y
z

wasp wasps
A **wasp** is an insect with black and yellow stripes. It has a sting.

waste wastes, wasting, wasted
When you **waste** something, you do not use it well.
You've wasted an hour finding your pen.
This food will be wasted if no one eats it.

watch watches, watching, watched
1 A **watch** is a small clock you wear on your wrist.
2 You **watch** someone by looking at them to see what they are doing.

water
Water falls from the sky as rain. It flows down rivers to the sea.

waterproof
If something is **waterproof**, it does not let in water.
Bring a waterproof coat in case it rains.

wave waves, waving, waved
1 You **wave** to someone by raising your arm and moving it about.
2 A **wave** is also a raised line of water that moves across the sea.
The surfer rode on a huge wave.

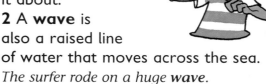

wax
Wax is a material. It is used to make candles and crayons. **Wax** melts when it is heated.

way ways
1 If you tell someone the **way**, you say how to get to a place.
2 The **way** to do something is how to do it.
This is the way to throw the ball.

weak weaker, weakest
Weak means not strong.
I ran up the hill till my legs felt weak.

wear wears, wearing, wore, worn
1 When you **wear** clothes, you have them on.
Ryan's wearing jeans today.
2 When something is **worn** out, it cannot be used any more.

weather
Rain, sunshine, storms and snow are different kinds of **weather**.
What's the weather like today?

web webs
A spider makes a **web** using threads that it makes in its body.
Spiders make webs to trap insects.

website websites
You look at a **website** on the Internet to find information.

wedding weddings
When two people get married, it is their **wedding** day.

Wednesday **Wednesdays**
Wednesday is the day of the week between Tuesday and Thursday.

weed **weeds**
A **weed** is a wild plant that people do not want in their gardens.

week **weeks**
A **week** is made up of seven days. There are 52 **weeks** in a year.

weekend **weekends**
Saturday and Sunday are called the **weekend**.

weigh **weighs, weighing, weighed**
Something that **weighs** a lot is hard to lift or carry. *An elephant weighs much more than a mouse.*

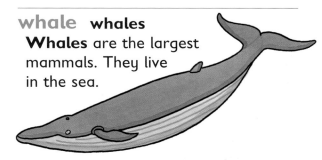

weight
The **weight** of something is how much it weighs.

well **better, best; wells**
1 If you do something **well**, you make a good job of it.
2 If you are **well**, you are healthy.
3 People get water out of a deep hole in the ground called a **well**.

wellington or welly **wellingtons or wellies**
Wellingtons are rubber boots. They keep your feet and legs dry.

went See **go**.

west
West is the direction you look when you see the sun set.

wet **wetter, wettest**
1 Something that is **wet** has water or liquid on it.
2 If the weather is **wet**, it is raining.

whale **whales**
Whales are the largest mammals. They live in the sea.

what
What is used to ask or talk about a thing.
*What is that? I can't see **what** it is.*

wheat
Wheat is a plant grown by farmers. Flour is made from its seeds.

wheel **wheels**
Cars, lorries and bicycles move along on **wheels**.

wheelchair **wheelchairs**
A **wheelchair** is a chair with wheels. It is used by someone who cannot walk.

when
When means the time at which something happens.
When are we going to the match?

a
b
c
d
e
f
g
h
i
j
k
l
m
n
o
p
q
r
s
t
u
v
Ww
x
y
z

a b c d e f g h i j k l m n o p q r s t u v **Ww** x y z

where

Where means the place at which something is.
*Where is my bag? It isn't **where** I left it.*

which

Which means the thing you have in mind.
*Which book have you chosen? Show me **which** one you like best.*

while

While means that two things happen at the same time.
*We went skating **while** we were in France.*

whisper whispers, whispering, whispered

If you **whisper**, you speak very quietly.

whistle whistles, whistling, whistled

1 You **whistle** by blowing air out of your mouth very loudly.
2 You can make the same noise using a metal or plastic **whistle**.

who

Who is used to ask or talk about a person.
Who put this frog on my chair?
*I'm the person **who** telephoned you yesterday.*

whole

The **whole** of something means every part of it.
*Janice ate the **whole** cake by herself.*

whose

Whose is used to ask or talk about the person something belongs to.
Whose pencils are these?
*She's the girl **whose** mother is a singer.*

why

Why is used to ask or talk about the reason for something.
Why are your shoelaces undone?
*That's **why** you fell over!*

wicked

A **wicked** person is evil. They do **wicked** things that are very unkind.

wide wider, widest

Something **wide** measures a long way from side to side.

width

When you measure how wide something is, you find its **width**.

wife wives

A **wife** is a woman that a man is married to.
*My gran is my grandad's **wife**.*

wild wilder, wildest

A **wild** animal or flower is one that lives without help from humans.

win wins, winning, won
The person who **wins** comes first in a race or competition.
*My team **won** the swimming race.*

wind winds
Wind is air that moves strongly and quickly.

windmill windmills
A **windmill** is a tower with large arms that are moved around by the wind. Farmers used to use power from a **windmill** to make flour.

window windows
A **window** is a hole in the wall that lets in light. **Windows** are often filled with glass.

windscreen windscreens
The driver of a car looks out through the **windscreen**. (See page 175.)

windy windier, windiest
It is **windy** when the wind is blowing more strongly than usual.

wing wings
A bird flaps its **wings** to help it to fly. An aeroplane's **wings** are fixed.

winner winners
The person who wins something is the **winner**.
*The **winner** of the first prize is Alfie.*

winter
Winter is the season between autumn and spring. It is cold and the days are short.

wipe wipes, wiping, wiped
If you **wipe** something, you clean it with paper or a cloth.
*Hayley is **wiping** the table.*

wire wires
A **wire** is a long, thin strip of metal. It bends easily and is used to fasten things. Fences and baskets can be made of **wire**.

wise wiser, wisest
A **wise** person knows a lot and is very sensible.

wish wishes, wishing, wished
1 If you **wish** for something, you want it very much.
2 When you make a **wish**, you hope to get what you want.

witch witches
A **witch** is a woman in stories who can do magic.

wives See **wife**.

a
b
c
d
e
f
g
h
i
j
k
l
m
n
o
p
q
r
s
t
u
v

Ww

x
y
z

wizard wizards
A **wizard** is a man in stories who can do magic.

wobble wobbles, wobbling, wobbled
If something **wobbles**, it shakes from side to side.
The jelly wobbled on the plate.

wobbly
If something is **wobbly**, it wobbles.

woke See **wake**.

woken See **wake**.

wolf wolves
A **wolf** is a wild animal like a large dog. **Wolves** live in groups called packs.

woman women
A **woman** is a grown-up female person.

won See **win**.

wonder wonders, wondering, wondered
When you **wonder** about something, you think about if it will happen.
I wonder if Gran will come today.

wonderful
Something **wonderful** is very good.
We've got a wonderful new TV!

won't
Won't is a short way of saying "will not".

wood woods
1 Wood is the material that comes from the trunks of trees.
2 A **wood** is a large group of trees.

wooden
Wooden means made from wood.

wool
A sheep's coat is made of **wool**. **Wool** is used to make clothes and blankets.

word words
You use **words** when you speak or write. A written **word** is a group of letters. It has a space at each side.

wore See **wear**.

work works, working, worked
1 Someone who **works** tries hard to do something.
2 When someone goes to **work**, they are going to do their job.

world worlds
The **world** is the planet that you live on and everything on it.

worm **worms**
A **worm** is a small slippery animal. It lives in the soil.

worn See **wear**.

worry **worries, worrying, worried**
If you **worry** about something, you are afraid that it might go wrong.

worse
Worse means more bad.
This film is even worse than last week's!
See **bad**.

worst
Worst means most bad.
This is the worst film I have ever watched!
See **bad**.

worth
1 Something is **worth** what you would expect to pay for it.
2 Something that is **worth** doing has a good result.

wound **wounds**
A **wound** is a cut or break in the skin.

wrap **wraps, wrapping, wrapped**
When you **wrap** something, you put something around it to cover it.

wriggle **wriggles, wriggling, wriggled**
If you **wriggle,** you move your body quickly from side to side.

wrinkle **wrinkles**
A **wrinkle** is a small fold.
Look at the wrinkles on that elephant!

wrist **wrists**
Your **wrist** is the place where your hand joins your arm. (See page 174.)

write **writes, writing, wrote, written**
You **write** when you put words on paper with a pen or pencil.

writing
When you have done some **writing,** you have written words on paper.

written See **write.**

wrong
1 Something **wrong** is not correct.
2 **Wrong** also means against the rules that people have made.
Telling lies is wrong.

wrote See **write**.

a
b
c
d
e
f
g
h
i
j
k
l
m
n
o
p
q
r
s
t
u
v
Ww
x
y
z

a b c d e f g h i j k l m n o p q r s t u v w
z

X-ray X-rays
An **X-ray** is a photograph of the inside of your body. It is taken using a special kind of light.

xylophone xylophones
A **xylophone** is a musical instrument. You play it by hitting wooden bars with sticks.

yacht yachts
A **yacht** is a sailing boat. People sail **yachts** for fun.

yawn yawns, yawning, yawned
You **yawn** by opening your mouth wide and breathing out noisily. You **yawn** when you are tired.
Tom yawned and said he was going to bed.

year years
A **year** has 365 days. There are twelve months in a **year**.

yell yells, yelling, yelled
You **yell** when you shout as loudly as you can.
The children were yelling with excitement.

yes
You say **yes** to show that you agree with something or that someone is right.
"I really like ice cream!" "Yes, so do I!"
"This is your coat, isn't it?" "Yes, it is."

yesterday
Yesterday was the day that came before today.

yogurt or yoghurt yogurts or yoghurts
Yogurt is a soft, thick food made from milk. It is often mixed with sugar or fruit.

yolk yolks

The **yolk** of an egg is the yellow part in the middle.

young younger, youngest

A **young** person or animal has not been alive for long.

your

Your means belonging to you.
*Is this **your** coat?*

yo-yo yo-yos

A **yo-yo** is a toy that goes up and down on a string.

zebra zebras

A **zebra** is an animal that lives in Africa. It is like a small horse with black and white stripes.

zebra crossing

zebra crossings

A **zebra crossing** is a place to cross the road. There are black and white stripes on the road.

zero zeroes

Zero is a name for the number 0.

zigzag zigzags

A **zigzag** is a line that bends suddenly up and down.

zip zips

A **zip** is a line of teeth that lock together to close something.

zoo zoos

Animals are kept in a **zoo** so that people can look at them.

a b c d e f g h i j k l m n o p q r s t u v w x

**Yy
Zz**

171

Dinosaurs

Brontosaurus was a plant-eating dinosaur with a long neck and long tail.

Tyrannosaurus rex was one of the largest meat-eaters, with very sharp teeth and claws.

Triceratops used its three horns to fight off other dinosaurs.

Pterodactyl lived at the same time as the dinosaurs.

Stegosaurus had bony plates on its back and a spiky tail to protect it.

Parts of the body

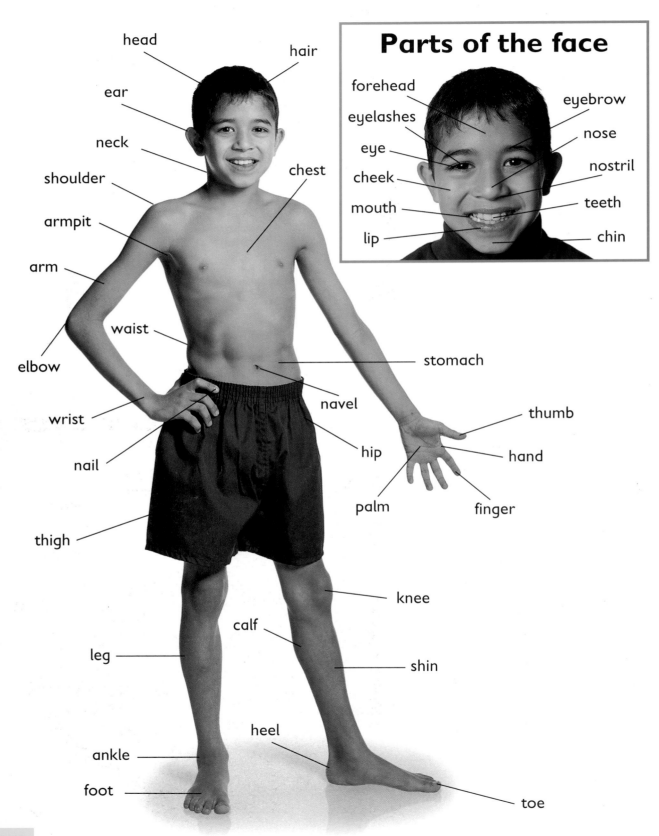

head

hair

ear

neck

shoulder

chest

armpit

arm

waist

elbow

stomach

wrist

navel

nail

thumb

hip

hand

palm

finger

thigh

knee

calf

leg

shin

heel

ankle

foot

toe

Parts of the face

forehead

eyebrow

eyelashes

nose

eye

nostril

cheek

mouth

teeth

lip

chin

Parts of a bicycle

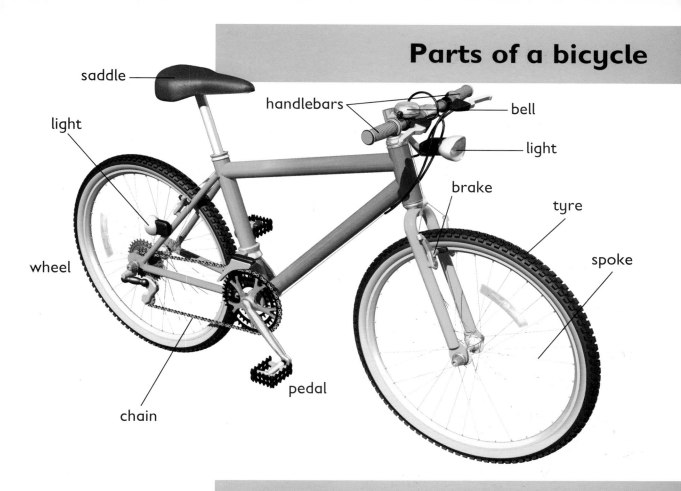

saddle

handlebars

bell

light

light

brake

tyre

wheel

spoke

chain

pedal

Parts of a car

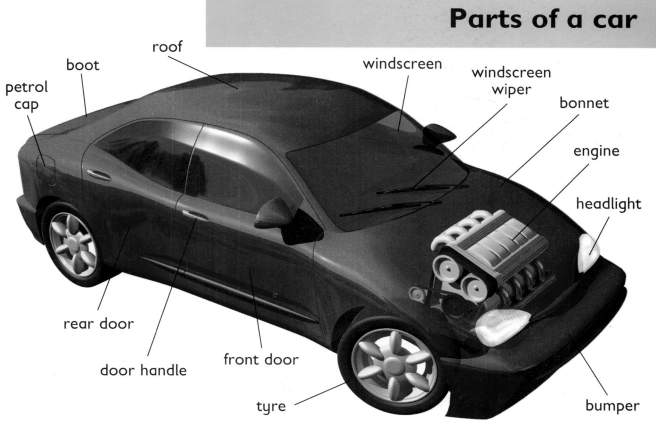

roof

boot

windscreen

windscreen wiper

petrol cap

bonnet

engine

headlight

rear door

door handle

front door

tyre

bumper

Clothes

blouse

scarf

dressing gown

nightdress

hat

jumper

jacket

skirt

glove

sandals

jeans

coat

tights

trainers

swimsuit

dress

knickers

slippers

leotard

Clothes

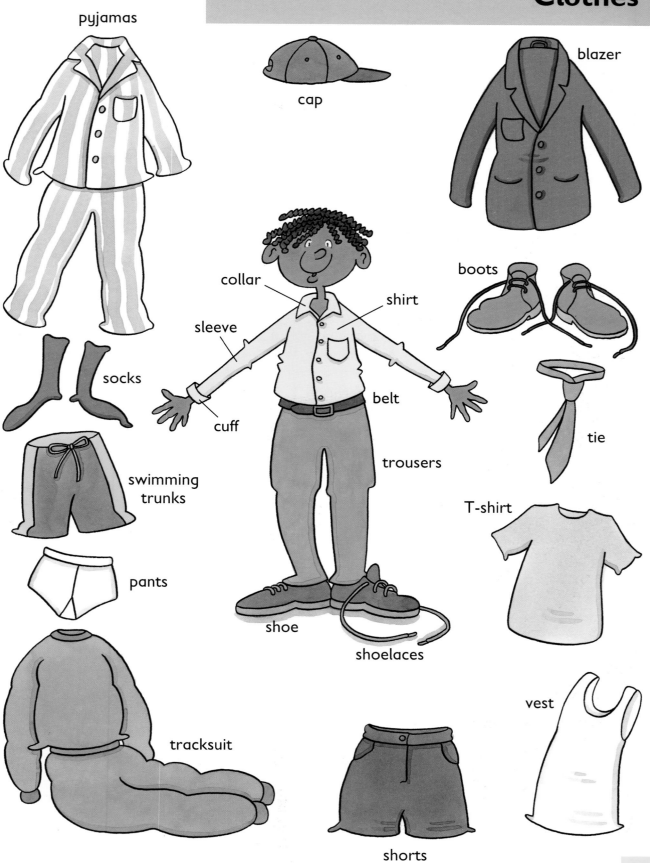

pyjamas

cap

blazer

collar

sleeve

shirt

boots

socks

cuff

belt

tie

swimming trunks

trousers

T-shirt

pants

shoe

shoelaces

vest

tracksuit

shorts

Time

one o'clock   quarter past one   half past one   quarter to two

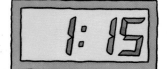

yesterday
today
tomorrow

second
minute
hour
day
week
fortnight
month
year
decade
century
millennium

dawn
morning
midday
noon
afternoon
dusk
evening
night
midnight

Days
Monday
Tuesday
Wednesday
Thursday
Friday
Saturday
Sunday

Months
January
February
March
April
May
June
July
August
September
October
November
December

Seasons

spring   summer   autumn   winter

Words we use to ask questions

how   what   when   where   who   why   which

Pronouns

I	me	my	mine	myself
you	you	your	yours	yourself, yourselves
he, she, it	him, her, it	his, her, its	his, hers, its	himself, herself, itself
we	us	our	ours	ourselves
they	them	their	theirs	themselves

Words we use a lot

a	can't	like	should
about	come	look	so
after	could	many	some
again	did	may	than
all	do	more	that
am	don't	much	the
an	for	must	then
and	from	next	there
another	get	no	these
are	go	not	this
as	going	now	to
at	got	of	too
away	had	once	very
back	has	or	was
be	have	out	way
because	here	play	went
been	if	put	were
but	in	said	will
by	into	saw	with
came	is	see	would
can	just	seen	yes

Synonyms

small
tiny …

big
large …

tasty
delicious …

neat
tidy …

wet
damp …

unhappy
sad …

yell
shout …

cook
bake …

afraid
scared …

fast
quick …

reply
answer …

18+7=25

Antonyms

Antonyms are words that mean the opposite.

sad   happy

high   low

wide   narrow

old   new

hot   cold

come   go

asleep   awake

full   empty

dark   light

inside   outside

open   closed

back   front

heavy   light

few   many

noisy   quiet

clean   dirty

soft   hard

wet   dry

fast   slow

Position words

up

down

top

first

bottom

through

last

above

below

between

on

off

over

far

beside

behind

under

near

in front

Numbers

0	zero	21	twenty-one	1st	first
1	one	30	thirty	2nd	second
2	two	31	thirty-one	3rd	third
3	three	40	forty	4th	fourth
4	four	41	forty-one	5th	fifth
5	five	50	fifty	6th	sixth
6	six	51	fifty-one	7th	seventh
7	seven	60	sixty	8th	eighth
8	eight	61	sixty-one	9th	ninth
9	nine	70	seventy	10th	tenth
10	ten	71	seventy-one	11th	eleventh
11	eleven	80	eighty	12th	twelfth
12	twelve	81	eighty-one	13th	thirteenth
13	thirteen	90	ninety	14th	fourteenth
14	fourteen	91	ninety-one	15th	fifteenth
15	fifteen	100	one hundred	16th	sixteenth
16	sixteen	200	two hundred	17th	seventeenth
17	seventeen	1000	one thousand	18th	eighteenth
18	eighteen	10 000	ten thousand	19th	nineteenth
19	nineteen	100 000	one hundred thousand	20th	twentieth
20	twenty	1 000 000	one million	21st	twenty-first

Measurement

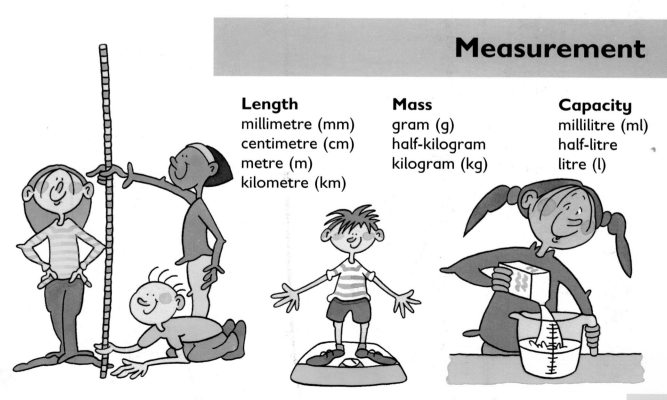

Length
millimetre (mm)
centimetre (cm)
metre (m)
kilometre (km)

Mass
gram (g)
half-kilogram
kilogram (kg)

Capacity
millilitre (ml)
half-litre
litre (l)

Shapes and colours

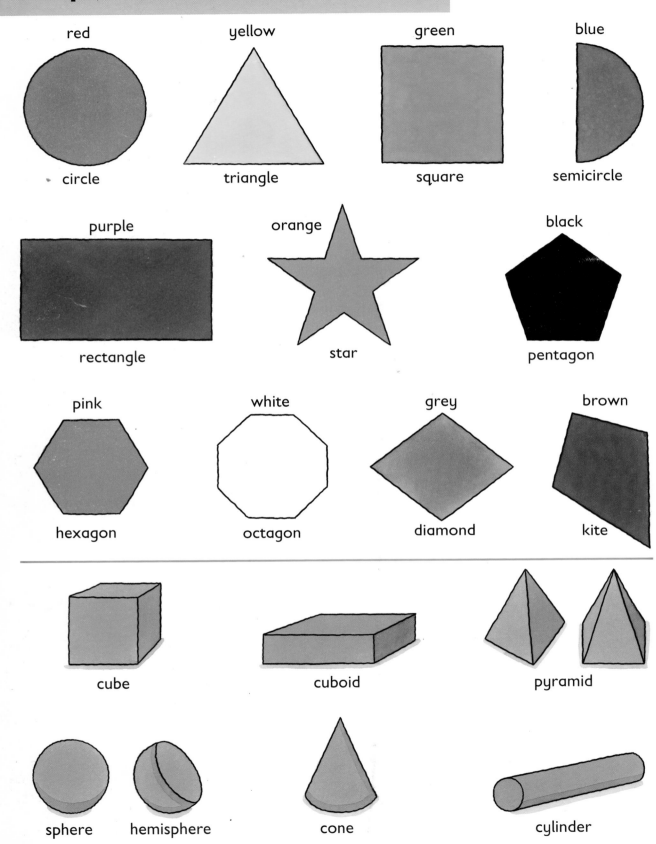

red — circle

yellow — triangle

green — square

blue — semicircle

purple — rectangle

orange — star

black — pentagon

pink — hexagon

white — octagon

grey — diamond

brown — kite

cube

cuboid

pyramid

sphere

hemisphere

cone

cylinder